RASA

RASA

Love Relationships in Transcendence

Swāmī B. V. Tripurāri

raso vai saḥ

Godhead is a reservoir
of transcendental
relationships

Clarion Call Publishing
Eugene, Oregon • Rome, Italy • Vrindavana, India

For more information about the Gaudiya Vaishnava Society, you may correspond with the secretary at:

Śrī Śrī Gaura-Nityānanda Audarya Āśrama
325 River Road
Eugene, OR 97404
USA
(503) 461-5760

Other Centers:

Rūpānuga Bhajan Āśrama
177 Rangaji Ka Nagla
Vṛndāvana, U.P. 281121
India

Śrī Kṛṣṇa Chaitanya Āśramam
Pandimuttam P.O.
Thiruvanthapuram
Kerala 645027
India

COPYEDITOR:
Vṛndāranya devī dāsī

DESIGNER:
Paurnamasi devī dāsī

COMPUTER ASSISTANCE WITH THE COVER:
Kayrin Gregory

Library of Congress
Catalog Card Number: 94-68581

ISBN 1-886069-10-7

Dedication

To Śrī Jīva Goswāmī,
who accepted with enthusiasm
the task of defending the position
of Śrīla Rūpa and Śrīla Sanātana
Goswāmīs, and who did so
eloquently and conclusively.

May he bless this
effort—an attempt to defend
the position of my spiritual masters,
Śrīla A. C. Bhaktivedanta Swami
Prabhupāda and Śrīla Bhakti
Rakṣaka Śrīdhara Deva Goswāmī,
by presenting the essence of their
conception in the language
of our times.

Abbreviations used in this book:

Bg.—*Bhagavad-gītā*

SB—*Śrīmad-Bhāgavatam*

BRS—*Bhakti-Rasāmṛta-Sindhu*

Cc. Adi—*Śrī Caitanya-caritāmṛta*
Adi-līlā

Cc. M.—*Śrī Caitanya-caritāmṛta*
Madhya-līlā

CONTENTS

ACKNOWLEDGMENTS

It would have been
impossible to have published
this book without the help of my
disciple Śrīmatī Vṛndāranya dāsī.

Her sincere effort
throughout, and especially
as our deadline approached,
has been a source of
inspiration.

May Śrī Chaitanya
bless her and the others who
directly and indirectly contributed
their effort to this project.

FOREWARD

Kṛṣṇa's pastimes in the ideal realm of Vṛndāvana are fresh and light in the poems that tell of them and the art that images them. It seems only fitting that writing, even theological writing, on devotion to Kṛṣṇa should reflect that freshness of spirit and lightness of touch, but rarely is this the case. Yet the first time I saw a draft of this book by Swāmī Tripurāri it was precisely these qualities that struck me and made me want to read further. His book moves quickly and surely, drawing the reader into a lively dialogue on what to make of the human predicament we share at the close of the twentieth century.

Perhaps we should characterize this book as an invitation to a debate among friends, for its author has some very definite points to make, free though he is of stridency and pedantry. Swāmī Tripurāri sets himself squarely within the Chaitanya Vaiṣṇava tradition of devotion *(bhakti)* to Kṛṣṇa. He writes from within a system of theology worked out by Jīva and Rūpa Goswamins in the sixteenth century and reaffirmed and restated by A. C. Bhaktivedānta Swāmī and Śrīdhara Swāmī in the twentieth. He presents the "good news" of Chaitanya's loving devotion *(prema-bhakti)* to Kṛṣṇa with directness and verve, with such apt contrast and analogies with other religious and cultural views and values as to challenge non-Vaiṣṇava readers to pay attention. Implicitly his is also challenging Vaiṣṇava readers to make good in practice the ideal promise of Kṛṣṇa *bhakti* for our times. His judgments are crisp and his proposals clear, as befits one who is confident and comfortable in the disciplic succession which he claims.

Not everyone will agree with all his judgments, but one readily sees the points he is making. They are good points, well worth amicable dialogue and debate. They help us face and formulate critical issues of life in personal and religious terms that bespeak hope, that offer explicit possibilities for living and loving in ways that are both humane and also devout.

The most striking claim of this book concerns the Kṛṣṇa-centered love that Chaitanya epitomized and sought to extend to all living beings. Swāmī Tripurāri argues that this Kṛṣṇa-centered love affirms and fulfills human sexuality while so channeling it and purifying it that it becomes a mode of God-centered spiritual experience. He claims that Chaitanya's mode of devout love for Kṛṣṇa is not only ontologically true but psychologically satisfying for human persons—for those wedded in conjugal love as well as for those who are celibate—and to an extent that neither materialistic lifestyles nor other religious ways of life can match.

This book does not attempt to prove this claim in any empirical or clinical fashion. What it does do, however, is challenge Kṛṣṇa-Chaitanya devotees to open their lives to the humanly fulfilling and spiritually transforming process of loving devotion *(prema-bhakti).* It also invites the rest of us to pay attention, to see if there really are signs among the devotees that *Kṛṣṇa-bhakti* does fulfill human life while purifying and spiritualizing consciousness and psychic experience.

One further thing that Swāmī Tripurāri's very readable book does is show how thoroughly grounded in Vaiṣṇava theology and in the scripture and literature of Kṛṣṇa-Chaitanya devotion is sacred love: love of Kṛṣṇa with his eternal servants, friends, kin, and consorts; Kṛṣṇa-centered love ideally embracing all living beings. Thus we find that it is the Kṛṣṇa-Chaitanya mode of loving devotion itself—and not just Swāmī Tripurāri's lively and timely exposition—that presents the real challenges and invitations to readers of this book.

Joseph T. O'Connell

Preface

One cannot be successful in spiritual life without the favor of the spiritual master, śrī guru. *My spiritual master asked me to distribute literature explaining the teaching of Śrī Chaitanya, especially in the Western world from where I hail.*[1] *By his grace, I was able to do so successfully, and it is by his grace that I am now able to write about the teaching of Śrī Chaitanya, explaining his doctrine from within the cultural context I am most familiar with.*

Let me offer my prostrate obeisances unto him, my eternal preceptor and ever well-wisher, Śrīla A. C. Bhaktivedanta Swami Prabhupāda, who is an ocean of compassion. Let me also offer my prostrate obeisances unto Śrīla Bhakti Rakṣaka Śrīdhara Deva Goswāmī Mahārāja, who at the request of my spiritual master has helped me immensely to understand the significance of the relationship between the guru and disciple as taught by Śrī Chaitanya. May they both bless the readers of this book, that the readers may one day soon relish the *prema-dharma* of Śrī Chaitanya and thus inspire me further along the path.

This book is very different from the style of the writings of my spiritual master. Yet it is written in the same bold spirit that possessed him to come to the Western world, which resulted, among other things, in my spiritual life.

1. The full name of Śrī Chaitanya is Śrī Kṛṣṇa Chaitanya. He is also referred to as "Mahāprabhu." "Mahā" is said to refer to mahābhāva, indicating Śrī Rādhā, and "Prabhu" refers to Kṛṣṇa, thus indicating that Śrī Chaitanya is the combined form of Rādhā-Kṛṣṇa. For consistency, I have chosen to refer to him as Śrī Chaitanya throughout.

Understanding to some extent the value of Śrī Chaitanya's teaching, I will consider this book successful if as a result of reading it even one person is moved even slightly in the direction of *prema-dharma.*

INTRODUCTION

The inspiration to write this book came to me in sacred Vṛndāvana, India in the autumn of 1989. After finishing the one month observance of the kārtika vrata *(a devotional vow observed for spiritual advancement), the gist of seven of the nine chapters of this book appeared in my mind. At that time, I was writing for, editing, and publishing an internationally circulated periodical about spiritual culture,* Clarion Call.

Clarion Call was directed to people of alternative culture who were both intellectually mature and spiritually inquisitive. The West has been experiencing a spiritual renaissance since the 1960s, which has also paved the way for pseudospiritual exploitation. *Clarion Call* addressed this spiritual hypocrisy while presenting India's ancient spiritual heritage in general and the teaching of Śrī Chaitanya, the deity of the Gauḍīya Vaiṣṇavas, in particular.

Caught up in addressing the mind-set of the spiritual seeker while living in the holiest of places, Śrī Vṛndāvana, I began to develop the chapters of this book. It is a book about just how different sexuality is from spirituality and how, ironically, the two, sex and the soul, are at the same time inseparable. Pure sexuality is the purest spirituality. The nine chapters that follow qualify this statement, distinguishing spirit from matter while establishing the novel idea that the soul has emotions and a sexuality of its own separate from the flesh. This is the precious gift of Śrī Chaitanya to the world.

In the first chapter, a brief historical overview of the Judeo-Christian influence on the way we have for centuries thought about sexuality is presented. This view is now unpopular, and many alternatives to it, both spiritual and mundane, have arisen to replace it. I have used Georg Feuerstein's terms of "body-negative" and "body-positive," as outlined in his book *Enlightened Sexuality,* to describe the traditional Judeo-Christian outlook (body-negative) and current alternative spirituality's outlook (body-positive).

Both the past from which many are turning and the future direction in which many are heading fall short of answering conclusively the question of our sexuality in relation to our spirituality. On this point the first chapter rests, clearing the path for a discussion about a truly sexually positive spirituality. In this chapter, I consider the sexuality and personhood of Godhead as found in traditional Western religion and his absence in monistic forms of Eastern spirituality.

This serves to further substantiate the idea that, ironically, both popular Christianity and all forms of monism, while seemingly radically different in their analyses of sexuality, are actually very similar. The concept of the personhood of Godhead, however, opens the door for the atomic soul to enter into transcendental relationship *(rasa).* In this relationship, the sexuality of the soul can be realized.

The best of alternative spirituality in the West leads to monistic transcendence, taking us beyond the dualities of the world of the five senses, mind, and intellect. As pervasive as this conception has become, gaining considerable influence even within Christianity, most people advocating the doctrine of "oneness" do not realize the import of what they are advocating. While pining for unity, they do not understand the philosophical ramifications of what it takes to realize oneness.

In discussing this confusion in the second chapter, I trace alternative spirituality to be drifting in the direction of the *advaita vedānta* of Ādi Śaṅkara. Here it is apparent that monism, while at a glance appearing to deliver us from a judgmental asexual uptight conception of God, has little to do with sexuality, the soul, or God.

While forms of monism and voidism may speak of sexuality in intellectually stimulating vernacular, as opposed to popular Christianity's overtly negative vernacular, it does little to liberate the soul's sexuality from the flesh, because it does not offer any information about the sexuality of the soul in transcendence. Monism and voidism are thus described as body-negative and soul-negative theologies. They are soul-negative because they do not afford the soul emotional fulfillment beyond embodied material life.

The third chapter is a glimpse into soul-positive and truly body-positive spirituality, which has little to do with the material body, but everything to do with the spiritual body and emotional fulfillment of the soul in transcendence. This chapter briefly overviews the philosophy of Vaiṣṇavism, or theistic, as opposed to monistic, *vedānta.* In this overview, the Vaiṣṇava conception of a personal God is presented in contrast to the conception of God that is missing in monism and underdeveloped in Christianity.

In discussing objectively the transcendentally progressive realizations of the Vaiṣṇava *ācāryas* over the advocates of voidism and monism, such as Buddha and Śaṅkara respectively, I have been careful to qualify the nature of the differences of such realizers. Their differences are much different from the warring factions of Saivaites and Vaiṣṇavites, Hindus and Muslims, Protestants and Catholics. The differences of realized souls are more than apparent differences. They are real differences based on viewing reality from different altitudes on the mountain of the absolute truth.

The fourth chapter is one of two that came to me only after writing the original seven chapters. I felt that in our scientific times, people would appreciate a presentation of the concept of a personal God and relationship with God in the language of logic and modern science. Monistic *vedānta* and Buddhism have been discussed in relation to quantum mechanics. This has been called the "new physics."

A famous example of new physics is Fritjof Capra's *The Tao of Physics.* David Bohm, renowned physicist and author of *Wholeness and The Implicate Order,* has stayed within a scientific framework more than Capra and most other authors who cross the line of science to dabble in spirituality. Therefore, I have referred to Bohm's book in discussing a spiritual world of love in a scientific context. In my discussion, I interface Śaṅkara's theory of *advaita vedānta* with Śrī Chaitanya's metaphysic of *acintya-bhedābheda.* The inspiration for this discussion came from Richard Thompson, author of *Mechanistic and Non-Mechanistic Science.*

In the fifth chapter, I discuss some of the many shortcomings of the empirical approach to knowing and establish hearing submissively from revealed scripture as a superior way of knowing. In establishing this concept, I discuss the Vedic evidence and arrive at Śrī Chaitanya's conclusion that the *Bhāgavata* is the ripened fruit of the tree of Vedic evidence. This is an important discussion, for it lays the foundation for discussing the theory of *rasa*, which is central to the *Bhāgavata* and thus is the essence of the Vedic wisdom. *Rasa* denotes the culmination of a doctrine of divine love—transcendental relationship with the personhood of Godhead and, ultimately, the fulfillment of the sexuality of the soul.

The sixth chapter opens the doors to Vaikuṇṭha, the Vaiṣṇava conception of the spiritual world, where Viṣṇu, "He who exists everywhere always," is served in awe and reverence *(vaidhi-bhakti)*. In this transcendental plane, the emotional potential of the soul is realized to some extent. Yet the regulated devotion of Vaikuṇṭha falls short of Śrī Chaitanya's teaching regarding the sexuality of the soul.

The seventh chapter introduces the doctrine of spontaneous love *(rāgānugā-bhakti)* as taught by Śrī Chaitanya. I included a brief biographical description of Śrī Chaitanya and the consensus of his followers as to his divinity. Kṛṣṇa, with his divine counterwhole Śrī Rādhā, is the divine couple of Śrī Chaitanya's adoration.[1] In the Kṛṣṇa conception of Godhead, divine love blossoms. Śrī Rādhā is understood to be the spiritual source of our sexuality *(hlādinī-śakti)*. Śrī Chaitanya personally shows the way to realize the truth of the sexuality of the soul through

1. Kṛṣṇa represents the *puruṣa* (predominating) or "masculine" aspect of Godhead. Śrī Rādhā represents the *prakṛti* (predominated) or "feminine" aspect of Godhead. Therefore, I have used "he" when referring to the predominating aspect of Godhead and I have used "she" when referring to the predominated aspect of Godhead. All other individual souls have also been referred to as "she." Although different from Śrī Rādhā, they are also predominated aspects of reality.

his advocacy of *kṛṣṇa saṅkīrtana,* congregational chanting of the names of Rādhā-Kṛṣṇa as found in the Hare Kṛṣṇa *mahā-mantra.*

Rasa is explained in greater detail in the eighth chapter. The self-evident nature of the teaching of Śrī Chaitanya is its beauty. *Rasa* culminates in what appears in the material world to be lawless (and thereby irreligious and nonspiritual) love. This revolutionary concept is called *parakīyā bhāva.* In human society to date, nothing higher has been told about the possibilities for loving relationship with Godhead. In this teaching lies the truth of the sexuality of the soul.

The last chapter, like the fourth chapter yet even more so, came to me as an afterthought. We live in postmodern times, and the *prema-dharma* (religion of divine love) of Śrī Chaitanya is the fulfillment of these times. It can save us from the frustration arising from the fact that we are now, after more than two centuries of so-called reason and enlightenment, morally and spiritually bankrupt. This frustration, although leading us away from senseless sense indulgence to a new and nonmaterial life, does not contain the potential to deliver a life of spiritual love. Śrī Chaitanya's *prema-dharma* does.

1

FROM BODY-NEGATIVE TO BODY-POSITIVE SPIRITUALITY

Postmodern times are at best moving us in a spiritual direction. As we are groping for a new model of life on which to place our feet firmly and move forward, the confusion that so characterizes postmodernism opens us to considering alternatives to outdated modernistic thinking. Hacker ethic, the idea that nothing is sacred and all things are open to be tampered with, is in one sense the direction that postmodern times are taking us, a direction that is not very appealing to the sensitive.

Yet when nothing is sacred and we have no fear to open any door, we may just open the right one and be surprised to learn that life itself is sacred and spirituality is our goal. Spirituality, humanity's greatest quest, will be attained neither by conquering the world of our senses nor by submitting to our present sensual demands, but by finding the source of our innate drive for love and embracing that love with all of our being. This spiritual love is, in a sense, the emotional fulfillment, even the sexuality, of our soul.

Georg Feuerstein has pointed out in *Enlightened Sexuality* that George Leonard was near the mark when in 1983 he said, "Sex . . . is an idea whose time has passed."[1] More accurately, we are getting past the fascination of genital sexuality. No doubt this is coming about gradually. Surely we are still thinking about sex, but the AIDS crisis and the spiritual vacuum created by self-centered genital sexuality

1. Feuerstein, Georg. *Enlightened Sexuality* (Freedom, CA: Crossing Press, 1989), Preface.

are two powerful influences that are helping to change the way we think about sex.

The popular image of the Madonna as a prostitute and a "material girl," represents only the surface of what has been called the sexual revolution. Underneath this sacrilege is a stirring of consciousness in search of deeper meaning in life. Now this consciousness is rising above the rejection of traditional religion's sexual mores and the embracing of a "no-holes-barred" sexual policy to a deeper understanding of our innate drive for love.

Many people who participated in the sexual revolution are concurring that the mystery of our sexuality cannot be solved outside a spiritual context. This is somewhat ironic, because religious convictions surrounding sex were the chains of repression the revolutionaries sought to break away from. We can't seem to get away from sex any more than we can God. Hundreds of scientific-industrial years of a love/hate relationship with God exploded into the orgasm of the sexual revolution. The post-industrial rhythm of the revolution has given birth to the child of fresh spiritual interest—unexpectedly.

The traditional Judeo-Christian worldview has for centuries determined our sexual attitudes. This traditional view of sex, at least on the surface, is not very different from the view of sex held by the majority of religions. It has been called a body-negative approach to spirituality, meaning that it is repressive and views the body negatively. Our society has been called body-positive, meaning that it places emphasis on the material body and has rejected many religious taboos. The body-negative approach has, understandably, seen its better days. Thus a resurgence of interest in spiritual life—a characteristic of the last decade of this century—is ushering in a new body-positive spirituality, and traditional Western religion has been saved from the threat of overpopulation.

Since the time of Peter and Paul, the Church has made it clear that God is good and sex is bad. Indeed, it goes all the way back to the Garden of Eden, where original sin was the Eve of Adam's eye. The Catholic Church officially accepted marriage only as a necessary evil. Sex for procreation was allowed, but the founding fathers openly preached the virtues of continent life. Paul himself, through whom marriage became acceptable, wrote, "It is a good thing for man to have nothing to do with women."[2] For Paul and his church, marriage was clearly second best.

For the sexually active, things got worse before they got better. Augustine, whose influence pervaded the Church for more than a thousand years, was antisexual to the extreme. Augustine found in the act of procreation the seed of original sin. He taught that Adam's sinful nature was biologically transmitted through procreation.[3]

It took a thousand years or so for the sexual repression of the Church to erupt into a volcano of protest. In fiery rhetoric, Martin Luther called compulsory celibacy the "handiwork of the Devil," when at age forty-two he married a twenty-seven-year-old nun.[4] Luther's new brand of Christianity gave marriage a positive status, and his style of Christianity with regard to sexual indulgence was contagious. Calvin, Zwingli, and a host of lesser reformers all followed suit with their own sexually permissive versions of Christianity. Yet the entire Protestant Reformation never went further than to encourage marriage over celibacy. Sanctified sex within marriage remained solely an act of procreation.

2. 1 Cor. 7: 1.

3. Vaughan, Frances. "Sexuality as a Sacrament: The Options of Spiritual Eroticism and Celibacy," *Enlightened Sexuality* (Freedom, CA: Crossing Press, 1989), p. 89.

4. Vaughan, "Sexuality," p. 91.

Today the Church has lost its grip on the congregation, which is no doubt influenced by the current of the sexual revolution even while condemning it. How many professed Christian men and women think twice today before having sex for pleasure in comparison to the days of Protestant reform? With examples like televangelists Jimmy and Tammy Baker and Jimmy Swaggart, no doubt many are daring to switch the channel to see what else is on the tube.

Pressure from feminists, homosexuals, and those concerned about AIDS is doing little to change the Church's stance on sexuality. A recent proposal to allow, among other things, practicing homosexuals access to the ordained ministry in the Episcopal Church was rejected by church fathers. President Bush, a practicing Episcopalian, commented on the proposal, "I'm not that liberal." Catholics also remain firm in their policy against contraception. Thus, new interest in religion in our sexually awake times is taking people outside the traditional boundaries of the Christian Church. As for those who are returning to the practice of Christianity, it is doubtful just how much of their sexuality they will leave behind.

Before discussing the now-popular body-positive alternatives of new Christianity, it will be helpful to first look at another aspect of Christian dogma, that of its monotheistic conception of the personhood of Godhead. In discussing sexuality and spirituality, it is important to consider the "sexuality" of the Godhead that any particular tradition posits. This may be the single most important consideration: Is God sexual?

Traditional Christianity's God the Father is absolutely asexual. Love for him is agape (Godly love), which has no similarity to the sexual love of man and woman. There is no similarity between agape and human sexual expression. God's "only begotten son" is thought to have entered the womb of Mary while keeping her virginity intact. The Son who became flesh is a figure we can pray to, surrender to. He is the love that God the Father expressed for us, the fallen souls, "For God so loveth the world that he sent his only Son."

Without Jesus, God's love and personhood remain abstract concepts. Jesus becomes the focal point as a personal God. Otherwise, God the Father's personhood is so obscure that he is often depicted by Christian fundamentalists with no face: "No man has seen the face of God and lived." But even so, Jesus the person we know very little about. We do not know if he was married or single or where he spent twelve of his thirty-three years on earth. What were his preferences, tastes, and mannerisms? Artistic license is unrestricted for those who attempt to depict him graphically, for there is no account of what he looked like.

Some may object to this type of questioning, for Jesus is to them, after all, God. But just what Christians mean when they say that God is a person is difficult to understand. Christianity insists that God is vaguely a person and we are his servants. This is very different from the concept of enlightenment found in most forms of Eastern spirituality. Christians cannot "become" God as the yogis supposedly can. Swāmī Vivekananda rocked the 1893 World's Parliament of Religions in Chicago when he told the audience, "You are looking for God, but you do not know that you yourselves are God." This is absolutely incompatible with traditional Christianity, yet the Church's explanation of God's personality, form, qualities, and activities in transcendence is so limited that it borders on absurd.

The Church's point that we are not God, either individually or collectively, is nonetheless a strong one, perhaps its strongest. If we are to talk about love, it makes sense that there must be enough separation between God and ourselves for there to be a reciprocal relationship. Love takes two. The concept of the personhood of Godhead requires bestowal of grace for our salvation. Prayer and surrender, the heart and love—not works or techniques—play the prominent role in the culture of Christianity's divine life. Yet unfortunately, the standard Christian explanation of God's personality, or better the lack of it, is practically self-defeating. To sin is to disobey this person, one who is by contemporary standards uptight and sexually repressed. Thus for many he is a myth that has long since seen its usefulness.

Most Christians continue to follow the strong sense within themselves that dictates that they are not God, but they do not stop to think about what the philosophical ramifications of a personal God are. For most, a personal God seems to mean a vague concept of God that each individual holds personally—you have your conception of God and I have mine. This is hardly getting to the bottom of what God is really all about, because it makes for a God that is no more than a product of the mind. Therefore, rational people are turning to other spiritual traditions and alternative explanations of Christ's teaching.

Matthew Fox, the Dominican priest who was recently silenced by the Church for one year, is prominent in the body-positive spirituality of alternative Christianity. Fox's "creation spirituality" calls for a renaissance of sexual mysticism. "The Cosmic Christ," writes Fox, "rejoices and is intimately at work and play when lovers make love. Angels flap their wings in envy at those times."[5]

Fox speaks of sex as the "original blessing" rather than original sin. His creation spirituality, as opposed to what

5. Fox, Matthew. *The Coming of the Cosmic Christ* (San Francisco: Harper & Row, 1988), p.164.

he calls fall/redemption spirituality, a term he uses to characterize the Church's body-negative stance, is molded after the philosophy of Meister Eckhart. Eckhart is still, after five centuries, under doctrinal scrutiny. Fox remains Christian in his own way, but it is questionable how long he will remain Catholic in the eyes of the Church. Fox's ecumenical leaning far outreaches that of Thomas Merton and other notable Catholic theologians.

Creation spirituality opens its arms to the popular trend toward reviving the best of our earth's pagan history. It also leans heavily on the East's prominent theme of nondualism, such that the personhood of God is almost dissolved into a new panentheism.[6] Panentheism posits that everything is in and of God, and that God is above everything as well. Yet Fox's version of panentheism places far greater emphasis on the creation being within God than the personhood of God that lives beyond the material creation. For Fox, finding the interconnectedness of all creation is tantamount to shaking hands with the Cosmic Christ.

Much of alternative Christianity is influenced by neopaganism. Shamans, witches, and matriarchal themes run throughout. Earth worship is tied to these teachings, making them environmentally sensitive. On the low end, alternative Christianity borders on paganism. It is a spirituality that makes no clear distinction between body and soul, heaven and earth. The culmination of this spiritual path is not devotion to a personal God, but a loosely described oneness with the earth or, in some cases, the cosmos. Sexuality is encouraged, often without restrictions or the requirement of "love" between partners. On the higher

6. Panentheism is not to be confused with pantheism. Panentheism, literally meaning "everything in God," is a term coined by K. C. F. Krause (1781–1832).

end of alternative Christianity, sex is encouraged for love and commitment as a way to find a wholeness that is absent in either the male or female alone. A fuzzy distinction between matter and spirit is made. The spiritual culture results in something similar to what the Hindus call *Brahman,* an undifferentiated state of conscious being, where personal self and ego disappear. On either end, the personhood of Godhead is usually reduced to a necessary but ultimately disposable focal point, a means to a higher impersonal end. Sexual love is considered agape when performed with some sense of spirituality in mind, however vague. References to erotic spirituality in the Christian tradition such as the Song of Songs in the Bible and Carmelite St. Teresa of Avila's bridegroom conception of Christ are often cited as justification for a body-positive outlook. Because in all of these alternatives Christ is central (at least in name), they are more readily turned to by Westerners in search of spirituality in our sexually liberated times.

A more radical departure from the norm is embracing Eastern spiritual traditions. Ancient Eastern philosophy is making an impact upon Western thought. This is so even as the East looks to the industrially developed West. Newly contrived Eastern spirituality has also made its appearance on the scene, making for many styles of meditation and yoga, most of which are sexually unprohibitive.

It is not that the mainstream of Eastern spirituality is sexually permissive. *Kāma* (sensuality) is clearly distinct from *prema* (love of God). Yet Hinduism and Buddhism speak of our sexual energy in different terms, ones that are more appealing to contemporary thinking. Even from within what might be called a body-negative spirituality, sex is spoken of in intriguing terms. Sexual energy's normal current toward genital orgasm is discussed in terms of reversing the tide and awakening higher centers *(cakras)* in the course of spiritual development. Thus the mystique of sex remains, even while genital sexuality is highly discouraged.

Some Buddhist and Hindu *tantric* traditions *(vāmāchāra)* do encourage genital sexuality, yet they are exceptions. They encourage genital sexuality under conditions of ritual as a means to enlightenment. Understandably, it is these traditions that lend readily to abuse. They represent only a fragment of the Hindu and Buddhist traditions, yet they are most popular in the new body-positive spirituality. Within the Hindu tradition, they were originally intended for those who were overly sensual and prone to intoxication, influenced by the darker mode of nature *(tamo-guṇa). Tantric* paths were a concession, not the norm. They have the same general goal as other Hindu and Buddhist paths, that of transcending sensuality and ego, and merging the individual with the cosmic ground of being, Brahman. This is thought to be accomplished by the cathartic effect of sensual immersion under the guidance of a guru. Yet in the West today, *tantric* is often heralded as the new way, and even as the true understanding of the diverse tradition of Eastern spirituality, an interpretation that works well with our so-called enlightened perspective on sexuality.

In all of the more popular interpretations of Eastern spirituality, there is inevitably no personhood to the Godhead. They advocate that we are that One, separated only by the illusion of separateness, ego. Yet they say many personal godly focal points appear to help us in our search beyond the limitations of form. Gods and goddesses abound, many of them appearing in sexually explicit postures, symbolizing the male and female poles, the yin and yang of life. These icons are meant to assist seekers in their search for balance and ultimately union beyond duality.

Whether it be an alternative Christianity or an Eastern spiritual discipline, the goal is to reach that state beyond form, beyond sex. Yet we have heard from alternative spirituality that sex is a positive spiritual influence, a beautiful blessing, even the very essence of our spirituality. Therefore, it is ironic to advocate, at the same time, an impersonal, voidistic, formless, and thus an even more asexual Godhead than that of traditional Christianity!

If after scrutiny we conclude that our sexuality in all its subtleties is integral to our being, there must be a truly sexually positive spirituality in which Godhead is not asexual. This cannot be a mental God, but one that all reason points to, leading us beyond reason's own limitations. This focus will bring about a normalizing and harmonizing of our sexual urge, such that it is understood in terms of its spiritual source. It will enable us to realize that whatever we find in illusion has its origin in reality. Thus a sexual, and thereby necessarily personal Godhead, both masculine and feminine, must come into focus.

The *Vedas* declare *raso vai saḥ.* The essence of life is *rasa,* love relationships in transcendence. *Raso vai saḥ* is a clarion call for transcendence beyond the constraints of genital sexuality, as well as beyond sexless, formless knowledge of *Brahman* or the Cosmic Christ, to a suprasexual transcendental relationship with Godhead. Such a divine personal Godhead is one with whom we can be one in purpose, thereby transcending duality. Duality is not created by individuality itself, but by interest separate from the whole. When our intent becomes one with the whole, we do not become the whole but enter a state of divine rapture—*rasa*. This state of divine rapture is the subject of this book. But before we delve deeply into this conception, it is prudent to discuss in more detail the popular quasi-monism, as well as actual monistic transcendence, which seems to be the best that today's body-positive spiritual thinkers have come up with in their quest for a sexually enlightened spirituality. Without doing so, it is impossible to understand the transcendental conception of rasa.

2

WISHFUL ONENESS AND MONISTIC VEDĀNTA

Until recently our cultural, racial, sexual, and other differences have outweighed the greater balance that we have in common. In days past, we were taught in school about past cultures, of other races we would never meet face to face, other than in war or if we somehow got on the wrong bus, and often about each other's sex behind closed doors for men or women only.

Today children's learning experience is different. They learn a new perspective on ancient cultures, as today's adults make movies reexamining history, searching out just where we went wrong. They ride the same bus and take lunch with different races or come themselves from mixed racial parenthood. They learn about male and female sexuality firsthand, as contraception has become the fact of life. They learn that we are interrelated with the ground we stand on, that to pollute the air, the water, or the earth is what it used to be to neglect to clean our room. In short, that which we have in common with our environment and one another is beginning to take precedence over superficial or misperceived differences. As this becomes the standard of common knowledge, uncommon men and women search for even greater common ground in the metaphysic of our being.

"One" we may be in many respects, but overcoming our differences for greater world harmony will not come from wishful thinking. Bette Middler's chart-topping song "From a Distance," in which she sings "God is watching us," "there is harmony," and "you look like my friend" is sensually appealing and emotionally moving poetry, but not much more. This and other sentimental ideas of unity and harmony all fall short when the push of our sensual demands comes to shove another from gratifying theirs. The bottom line of our differences is drawn by our instruments of perception, the senses. The five senses and the mind create the material duality of "yours" and "mine." Anything short of withdrawing our senses from their present preoccupation with sense objects will do little to bring unity to the world. If we want to solve the mystery of how to bring about unity, we will have to become mystics, from the Greek *mystikos,* meaning "quiet the senses and enter the mysteries."

Ebbing the tide of our sensual current that flows like a great river into the experiential ocean of touch, taste, smell, sight, and sound is just the beginning of spiritual life, however. If we stop there, we are left with the damming effect of body-negative spirituality. At any moment the dam could burst. Moving upstream to a body-positive spirituality involves much more than merely suspending our senses. Yet it cannot be over emphasized that "body-positive spirituality" is only an oxymoron unless we check the perpetuation of material existence resulting from sense perception.

Ancient India's *vedānta* explains conclusively how a worldview arrived at from material sense perception is the antithesis of spirituality. In the *Bhagavad-gītā,* we find,

mātrā-sparśās tu kaunteya
śītoṣṇa-sukha-duḥkha-dāḥ

"The duality of happiness and distress, hot and cold, and all such opposites are merely a perception created by the five senses and the mind." (Bg. 2.14) With our hands we touch the world. With our tongue we taste flavors. With our nose we smell aromas. With our eyes we see form.

With our ears we hear sound. These are the instruments of perception that contact the world and relay messages to the mind. The mind in turn determines the good or bad of any experience relative to our sensual particulars. Through the senses and the mind we create our own reality, yet by no means do we understand the truth. What is "good" for you may be "bad" for me. In this way, the separateness of material duality is created, and unity is not at hand.

With the help of sound reasoning, it is possible to rise somewhat above this dilemma. We may, for example, feel that something is good yet know with our intellect that it is not good for us. The intellect sits above the mind, senses, and sense objects. As the *Bhagavad-gītā* tells us, *indriyāṇi parāṇy āhur indriyebhyaḥ paraṁ manaḥ manasas tu parā buddhir.* (Bg. 3.42) With the help of our intellect, our discriminating faculty, we can come closer to the nature of reality. The intellect should regulate the senses and the mind. All three of these aspects of our embodied life must function properly in terms of their status in a hierarchical system, for when the intelligence gives way to the demands of the mind and senses, it is as though the vehicle of our body is without its driver. Yet we are not a driver of bodily demands, nor are we a material body. We are a passenger, the self. The self is not a composite of body, mind, and intelligence, but an entity unto itself, that which gives meaning and purpose to the vehicle (the body) and its driver (the intellect).

The intellect points ultimately to its own limitations. The rational world of the intellect is prim and proper, regulating our mental and sensual demands and bringing us out of the jungle of unrestricted sensuality. Such a reason-ruled life is certainly more accommodating than a bestial existence, yet it has its constraints. It is, in one sense, a life of constraint. Without knowledge or experience of pure consciousness, the self is ever pushing for the love that is blind to reason, the love of the senses. Yet if there is a life beneath reason, there must be a life above reason as well. This is spiritual life, a life that retires the calculating "proceed-with-caution" reason-guided tour of sense control. This is the life of the soul, the life of love. Yet again, if we remain tied to the demands of the senses and mind, we walk a life of love only in our imagination.

The wishful oneness sought by many today is not very well thought out. Not only will it never be realized as long as the senses remain our guides, but if we do manage to move systematically beyond the duality arising out of sense perception, what is it that we will be united for? After all, the world is for the most part united in its interest in sense indulgence, yet this unity is problematic. Therefore, unity for what is the more important question. If it is unity for nothing (voidism) or unity in which there is no other (monism), there is little scope for love. Is that really in our interest?

To answer these questions, it is necessary to discuss "enlightenment" as it is characterized within *advaita* (monistic) *vedānta.* In doing so, it should become apparent that the popular drift toward oneness leads ultimately to *advaita-vedānta,* although in most cases the philosophical ramifications of *advaita-vedānta* are not understood. Once the philosophical ramifications are clarified, it should be apparent that this philosophy, although describing a state of experience beyond the constraints of the body, mind, and intellect, is one in which unity is all for naught. This is so because while the price for such unity is abandoning lust, the purchase is not the fullest expression of love. To make clear the philosophical ramifications of nonduality, it is helpful to discuss *advaita-vedānta* in light of its foremost proponent, Ādi Śaṅkara.

Śaṅkara (788-820 C.E.) lived only thirty-two years, yet his contribution to the world is immeasurable. He renounced the world at age twelve and soon thereafter wrote his famous commentary on the *Vedānta-sūtras*, called *Śārīraka-bhāṣya* or *Naiṣkarmya-siddhi*. This commentary established his *advaita-vedānta* school so firmly in the Indian subcontinent that the then prominent Buddhist doctrine was effectively driven out of India.[1] Although Śaṅkara's doctrine of nondualism is very similar to the voidism of the Buddha, Śaṅkara relied heavily on the Vedas to assert his view. Buddhism, on the other hand, is *nāstika*, unaccepting of the Vedic literature, and openly atheistic.

Today there are many shades of Buddhism and *advaita-vedānta*, such that the two are often thought to complement one another. Yet at the time of Śaṅkara's incarnation, his original *advaitin* doctrine was distinct from the teaching of the Buddha. While Buddhism is soulless *(anātman)*, *advaita-vedānta* posits a soul—one soul. While Buddhism is atheistic, *advaita-vedānta* rides the fence between theism and atheism.

In the *Padma Purāṇa*, we find the following description of Śaṅkara:

māyāvādam asac-chāstraṁ
pracchannaṁ bauddham ucyate
mayaiva vihitaṁ devi
kalau brāhmaṇa-mūrtinā

Śiva informed his wife, "In Kali-yuga I incarnate as a *brāhmaṇa* and explain the Vedas such that my conclusions amount to a covert form of Buddhism." Thus while speaking of God *(īśvara)*, which Buddha never did, Śaṅkara ex-

1. Narasingha Mahārāja. *Evolution of Theism* (Vṛndāvana, India: GVS, 1989), p. 21.

plains God away, claiming that we are all God, *tat tvam asi.* "Thou art that." God is really missing here, inasmuch as there can be no supreme being without subordinates. If the devotee is in actuality God, then neither God nor the devotee actually exists, nor does the world, offers Śaṅkara in his famous statement, *brahma satyam jagat mithyam.* "Consciousness is real, the world is false." Thus, Śaṅkara's philosophy concludes that there is no *īśvara* (God), no *jīva* (atomic soul), and no *jagat* (objective world)—all is *Brahman* (consciousness); all is one, *advaita.* These are some of the philosophical ramifications of nondualism often not considered by those who only wishfully dream about oneness while remaining in the world of the senses.

Śaṅkara's logic is powerful. It brings us beyond the wishful oneness of those who only dream about unity. The world of sense perception is fleeting and dreamlike—here today and gone tomorrow, never to appear again. The movement of consciousness within the jurisdiction of the sense world is reactionary. Action here bears the fruit of reaction *(karma),* which is binding *(saṁsāra).* Knowledge is that which takes us beyond the mortality of the plane of sense perception. With the culture of knowledge, it is understood that everything we perceive with our senses is deceiving and will not endure. Thus *vairāgya* (detachment or renunciation) is the symptom of one who has real knowledge. Knowledge destroys the impetus to act as it reveals the nature of such activity to be binding. When action ceases and the reactions of previous *karma* are exhausted, *saṁsāra* (bondage) ceases. It sounds simple, but we cannot wish or think our way there. First we have to stop thinking, to still the mind. Any genuine spiritual discipline culminating in the experience of undifferentiated consciousness or the similar goal of the many Buddhist sects, is a life-consuming process. The goal is not cheap.

Is this the direction in which the movements of popular oneness are moving? Yes and no. Yes, because the strong sense of our interconnectedness, our oneness, comes from the fact that we are all consciousness, *Brahman,* not African, Indian, or American; male or female. No, because the philosophical ramifications of this reality are not a topic of discussion, and thus the methods for realizing this truth are not being employed. Once the philosophical ramifications of monism are understood, a bigger question arises: Is the oneness of monism or voidism really desirable? Here again, yes and no. If our spirituality ends with Śaṅkara's *Brahman,* no. If nonduality is foundational to the further development of our spiritual life and love of God, yes.

Rising above the dualities generated from sense perception makes for firm footing in a nontemporal life. Thus we do not want to do away with nonduality, but there is more to nonduality than monists think. Although some of the harshness of Śaṅkara's "consciousness is truth, the world is false" monism has been softened by realizers such as the late Ramaṇa Mahārṣī, contemporary teacher Da Free John, and others, all these teachers settle for much less than what a nondual life is potentially about. Nonduality can be the basis for a life of body-positive and soul-positive spirituality.

Even Da Free John's and Rajneesh's self-styled radical *tantric* approaches, which appear to be sex-positive, are ultimately body-negative, and thus sex-negative. The process for transcending the senses is different than in other traditions, but the goal is the same—to be sexless and formless. Otherwise, Śaṅkara and the host of spiritual teachers in the monistic traditions all strongly advocate celibacy and renunciation.

Monism and voidism are soul-negative, because in these traditions the *jīva* (individual atomic soul) ceases to exist or exists only in illusion. For the voidist there is no soul. As for the monist, although one soul is admitted, many souls are not. This can be construed as soul-negative if we look to the soul-positive and body-positive *(siddha-deha)* teachings of Rāmānuja, Madhva, and ultimately Śrī Chaitanya, all of who taught theistic, or Vaiṣṇava *vedānta.* These Vaiṣṇava schools are soul-positive because they admit to the eternal individuality of the atomic soul. They are body-positive because they teach that the soul ultimately has a spiritual form *(sac-cid-ānanda vigraha).* They are also body-positive in a lesser sense because they do not advocate repressing the senses or denying them, nor do they advocate excessive indulgence of the senses as found in the many *tantric* traditions. Instead they advocate employing the body in the service of Godhead.

3

BEYOND MONISM

Indian philosophy is hardly the monolith of monism it is often made out to be. Vedic monotheism preceded monism in India. The Padma Purāṇa *speaks of four ancient Vaiṣṇava lineages, and after Śaṅkara's monistic contribution, theists such as Rāmānuja, Nimbārka, Viṣṇu Swāmī, and Madhva established devotional traditions based on the* Vedānta-sūtras.

There are many saints in Indian history. Yet most of them did not establish entire schools of thought. This is so the world over. Saints of varying realization appear and disappear, leaving us with glimpses of the spiritual dimension. Many never leave any writings behind. Their greatness cannot be underestimated, but those who have established traditions of religious thought are greater still. In the Indian tradition they are called *ācāryas.* Discussing their contributions to religious thought is helpful, because they have systematized and crystallized their realizations into a form that we can best take advantage of. It is for this reason that when introducing the topic of monism Ādi Śankara must be mentioned. When discussing Buddhism, Gautama; Christianity, Christ; yoga, Pātanjali. Along the *vedantic* line of thought from Śaṅkara, the luminaries Rāmānuja and Madhva are highly significant. Rāmānuja qualified the realization of Śaṅkara with his *viśiṣṭhādvaita* philosophy, and Madhva took it a step further when he introduced his *dvaita* devotional tradition. These traditions are soul-positive and body-positive forms of theism. While Śaṅkara rode the fence between atheism and theism, Rāmānuja and later Madhva stood firmly on the side of theism. In their *ṭīkās (vedantic* commentaries), the shortcomings of Śaṅkara's *advaita-vedānta* are thoroughly discussed.

The differences between great spiritual teachers, however, should not be misconstrued. They differ in their descriptions of the absolute only because of being situated in varying degrees of penetration into that infinite subject. Differences also arise when one speaks not solely of one's realization, but of what others at the time might best benefit from. A school teacher writes ABC on the blackboard, yet she herself can write a whole book. Her students should not think that she knows only the ABC's.

The differences between great spiritual luminaries are not like the differences among warring factions of fundamentalists. The general populace adopts popular versions of genuine religious truths. Truth will never be popular in a place where untruth, illusion, is the standard fare. In the material world, illusion is the language we speak. Addressing one another as Indian, American, red, black, white, yellow, man, or woman, we speak only of and to an illusory sense of self. We address only the material conditioning of one another without understanding who we really are. When the discussion turns to the "spiritual," the same applies. Whether it be Hindu, Muslim, Catholic, Protestant, Jew, or so on, the discussion hovers around the externals of the particular tradition at best. This often deteriorates into "religious" discussions that add up to no more than politics. The essential conclusions of these traditions are not central to the talks that sometimes turn to terrorism.

The simple reason for this is that the vast majority of people are externally oriented and steeped in illusion, even while adopting a spiritual path. Divinity descends even while we are looking in the opposite direction. It does so through conventional forms of expression. Otherwise we would not be able to understand the divine at all. Just as we cannot hear a high-pitched dog whistle because our hearing is not sensitive enough, similarly we cannot heed the clarion call of Godhead unless it is broadcast on the frequency to which we are tuned. Even then, we hear only partially. Although it is our self-interest that Godhead addresses, we do not care that much about ourselves. How can we, when we do not even know who we are? This is our sorry plight, one for which no one is to blame but ourselves.

Yet in every spiritual tradition there are those who are able to perceive the inner meaning. These esoterists embrace religion experientially. They do not differ with one another in the same way as the beginners, who often are so prone to superficial understanding that they even reject those great experiencers who hail from their own sect. The Jews rejected Jesus, the Hindus of Nadia rejected Śrī Chaitanya. But the great experiencers do differ. Because their experience is sublime, peaceful, blissful, ecstatic, mystic, and beyond the senses, their differences are not expressed in terms of the senses. They do not come to blows over whether *Brahman* is without quality, as in Śaṅkara's abstract monism, or has qualities, as in the case of Rāmānuja's concrete monism. But they do differ, and addressing these differences with objectivity will take us up the ladder of divinity without insulting anyone along the way. Discussing the contributions of the great realizers is helpful in terms of conceptually embracing the highest ideal, but we should always keep in mind where we are on the great mountain of the absolute. We must remember that those luminaries who have gone before us have not stopped where their teachings seem to.

One basis for an objective discussion of abstract monism versus concrete monism, or monism versus transcendental dualism, is the Vedic evidence. The *vedantic* schools of thought are based on an understanding of the *Vedānta-sūtras* of Kṛṣṇa Dvaipāyana Vyāsa. These *sūtras*, or codes, form what is called *nyāya-śāstra*, or the logic of *vedānta*. If you do not have a commentary on the *Vedānta-sūtras*, you do not have your own school of *vedantic* thought. Rāmānuja's commentary is the *Śrī-bhāṣya*, written in the eleventh century C.E. His commentary was the first to challenge the understanding of Śaṅkara successfully.

According to Śaṅkara, nothing exists except *Brahman*, a changeless, formless eternity that is devoid of qualities. For Śaṅkara, the world does not exist. Rāmānuja felt that this notion of Śaṅkara was more akin to fiction than was the world. An ultimate reality that is indeterminate, without attributes, is meaningless. Any reality that cannot be perceived, thought of, known, or talked about is not very real. The world, according to Rāmānuja is not the ultimate reality, but it does exist. It is not real, in that it is not the truth—just as when a magician creates an illusion. What he creates is not real, yet the illusion itself is. Illusion for Rāmānuja is to perceive something to be other than what it is. But for Rāmānuja, material nature is a real influence resulting in misperception, not, as Śaṅkara would have us believe, something that ultimately does not exist at all.

The *Vedānta-sūtras* inform us: *oṁ janmādy asya yataḥ*. This asserts, according to Rāmānuja, that the truth, Godhead, is that from which all things emanate. It does not say that the truth is that from which the illusion of "things" (the world) is generated, as Śaṅkara claims.

Rāmānuja recognizes a unity of three categories: individual units of consciousness *(cit)*, matter *(acit)*, and Godhead *(īśvara)*. These three categories are related by way of the individual units of consciousness and matter being the attributes of Godhead. There is a unity between the individual units of consciousness, matter, and Godhead, yet there is a distinction between them as well. Just as the soul remains changeless as the body undergoes transformation, so the world and the individual souls undergo transformation while Godhead remains undisturbed. The world and the individual units of consciousness are not nonexistent as Śaṅkara would have us believe, but are aspects of Godhead, *viśiṣṭhādvaita.* With the understanding that the devotee *(cit)* and Godhead *(īśvara)* are distinct aspects of the nondual *Brahman,* the door opens for a philosophy of genuine devotion. The devotee serving Godhead in knowledge represents healthy interaction between the individual units of consciousness and Godhead. When the individual soul is materially conditioned and in ignorance of Godhead, an unhealthy relationship between the individual units of consciousness and matter results, wherein the individual soul attempts to exploit the material nature, ignoring that both the individual soul and the material nature are aspects of Godhead intended for his purpose alone.

Rāmānuja explained that just as the material body we now experience is a manifestation of our impurity or ignorance, so in pure consciousness a body suitable for love of God is manifest. Our present material body is a product of ignorance. This must be so, because from it we derive so much suffering. The pleasure of the material body amounts to not much more than temporarily alleviating the suffering that the material body and its background of distorted consciousness bring on. Because the material body manifests only temporarily, even if we like it, we cannot keep it.

Śaṅkara also tells us that the material body is temporary, but he stops there. Because the material body and the material manifestation itself bring about misery for the soul, the formlessness of monism sounds liberating. Yet without form and individuality there is no scope for relationship, which we so desperately seek. But we want relationship with matter, over whom we think we can be the Lord. However, because individual souls and matter are dependent aspects of Godhead, our prospect for a meaningful relationship lies in Godhead, wherein we are a servant, rather than in a relationship with matter, wherein we think we are the Lord.

Madhva speaks of the same God as Rāmānuja. His theistic *vedānta* is called *dvaita* (dual). Madhva's philosophy of duality is not the duality that arises from sense perception. Rather, his philosophy describes the nature of being as perceived from a transcendental vantage point. According to the simple logic of contradictions, "A" is not "B," and "A" is not "not B," we can come up with as many strong arguments for reality being nondual as we can for the case of duality. Madhva did so. He forcefully asserted that the living entities and Godhead are eternally different from one another.

Madhva perceived five absolute and eternal differences: the distinction between God and the finite souls, between God and the inanimate world of matter, between one finite soul and another, between the finite souls and matter, and between one inanimate object and another.

Thus for both Rāmānuja and Madhva there is enough difference between God and ourselves for there to be a spiritual life of love in which the personality of Godhead is the center. In their versions of Vaiṣṇava *vedānta,* the unity, which all souls sense is at the heart of truth, is realized without the necessity of compromising the diversity, which makes life worth living. As already explained, monism and voidism leave little room for an enlightened life of love. The difference between voidism and monism can be summed up in Shakespeare's famous line, "To be or not to be, that is the question." Voidists choose not to be *(anātman),* while monists choose to be *(brahma-nirvāṇa),* but unlike Shakespeare's Hamlet, they choose to be alone as the only soul in undifferentiated oneness. Vaiṣṇava *vedānta* saves us from either of these alternatives, which although very different, are also pretty much the same. There is not much difference between not being and being alone forever. While Śaṅkara's monism takes us to the shore of the ocean of truth, Rāmānuja and Madhva push us in. Monist Ram Dass' famous book *Be Here Now* is only a small part of the picture. There is more to spiritual life than merely being or existing. We exist for something—to love. Chaitanya Vaiṣṇavite visionary Swāmī B. R. Śrīdhara gives us a glimpse into the full picture of transcendental life in his poetic remark, "Love does not want to see into the future, but only the present—the concentrated present. Love. For love we may risk the whole future and may not care at all about the past. Act. Act in the living present."[1]

1. Swami B. R. Sridhara. *Sermons of the Guardian of Devotion* (North Yorkshire, UK: The August Assembly, 1988) Vol. III, back cover.

4

From Physics to the Metaphysics of a Personal God

For India's great realizers, the primary evidence in support of their theses is revealed scripture (śāstra), *such as the* Vedānta-sūtras. *This evidence is considered to originate beyond the limits of human reasoning. Yet, especially for Westerners, as an introduction to the virtues of scriptural evidence, it may be prudent to first discuss the concept of a transcendental personal Godhead in the context of modern science and quantum mechanics in particular.*

In the transition from Newtonian classical physics to quantum mechanics, several scientists have explored the possibility of a connection between physics and transcendence. This may be due to the more abstract nature of quantum mechanics as opposed to classical physics. For example, classical physics attempts to describe the physical reality in concrete, easily understandable terms, while quantum mechanics deals in probabilities and wave functions. Quantum mechanics, however, is much more rigorous in its attempt to describe reality and it explains phenomena that classical physics fails to account for. The "quantum leap" has given several physicists the hope that the transcendentalist's experience of consciousness can be explained by quantum mechanical theory. Although quantum theory does not account for consciousness, it has become popular to attempt to bridge the gap between the transcendentalist's experience and the quantum mechanic worldview. Some people have loosely called this attempt the "new physics."

The rational, spiritually minded community cheered the appearance of Fritjof Capra's *The Tao of Physics* and Gary Zukav's *Dancing Wu Li Masters*. Several years later, David Bohm's *Wholeness and the Implicate Order* was similarly praised. Although there is good reason to applaud these authors' work and the work of others like them, their theories, scientifically speaking, do not bridge the gap between physics and transcendence. However, these scientists have to some extent become "believers," and their theories have turned many educated people in the spiritual direction.

Of all the recent attempts to show the "oneness" in what physicists and transcendentalists speak of, Bohm's implicate order theory is the most worthy of consideration. In comparison, Capra's "realization" that the dance of Śiva and the movement of atomic particles is one and the same—although profoundly beautiful—falls more in the realm of poetry than science.

Bohm's explanation of reality involves what he calls an "implicate" and "explicate" order, with vague references to love, compassion, and other similar attributes that may lie beyond both the implicate and explicate orders. The implicate order is the ultimate reality, which underlies our present perception of the world. The reality that we perceive is what Bohm calls the explicate order. All order and variety, according to Bohm, is stored at all times in the implicate order in an enfolded or unmanifested state. Information continually unfolds, or becomes manifest, from the implicate order as the explicate order of our experience.

Bohm uses the example of the hologram to help explain his theory. A hologram is a photographic plate on which information is recorded as a series of density variations. Because holography is a method of lensless photography, the photographic plate appears as a meaningless pattern of swirls. When a coherent beam of light—typically a laser—interacts with the plate, the resultant emerging light is highly ordered and is perceived as an image in three dimensions. The image has depth and solidity, and by looking at it from different angles, one will see different sides of the image. Any part of the hologram will reproduce the whole image (although with less resolution). Bohm would say that the three-dimensional form of the image is enfolded or stored in the pattern of density variations on the hologram.

A further understanding of the nature of Bohm's implicate order is somewhat more difficult to grasp. In the transition from the classical description of physical objects to a quantum mechanical description, one is forced to use mutually incompatible descriptions. The concept of complementarity, conceived of in the 1920s by the physicist Niels Bohr, says that to understand the behavior of electrons, it is necessary to describe them as pointlike particles and extended waves. This leads naturally to the thought that electrons or their ultimate substrate, may not actually be fully describable in mathematical terms. Thus the ultimate physical reality may be only partially definable, because some of the partial descriptions will inevitably contradict each other. This is Bohm's idea regarding the nature of his implicate order.

Although Bohm accepts a whole containing distinguishable parts, he maintains that ultimately reality is fundamentally devoid of variety or individuality. Bohm believes that individuality is a temporal or illusory state of perception. According to his theory, although the parts appear to be distinct from the whole, in fact, because they "enfold" or include the whole, they are identical with the whole.

The hologram provides an easily understandable example. If portions of a hologram are blocked off, the resultant image remains basically the same. This helps to illustrate metaphorically the concept that the whole is present in each of its parts. Consider, then, a continuum in which all patterns ever manifested in any part of the continuum are represented equally in all parts. Loosely speaking, one could then say that the whole of the continuum in both space and time is present in any part of the continuum. If we invoke the precedent of quantum mechanical indefinability, we could leap to the idea of a unified consciousness encompassing all space and time in which each part of the consciousness contains the whole of the consciousness and thus is identical to it.

Although Bohm's theory of the implicate order is partially based on the standard methodology of physics, it is also apparent that it involves ideas not found in traditional science. Most of these ideas are clearly the influence of a preconceived notion of nondualism. Richard Thompson, author of *Mechanistic and Non-Mechanistic Sciences,* has brought out some of the weaknesses in Bohm's theory, which he feels are due to Bohm's prejudice toward monism.

Thompson points out in his critique that while Bohm emphatically states that it is not possible for unaided human thought to rise above the realm of manifest matter (explicate order), he proceeds to carry on a lengthy discussion about the unmanifest (implicate order). Bohm also states that all things are timeless and unitary, and therefore incapable of being changed. Later, he proposes that through collective human endeavor the state of affairs can be changed. This is similar to the contradiction of *advaita-vedānta* in which ultimate oneness is thought to be *attained* even though it is beyond time and is forever uninfluenced by our actions.

Bohm's theory is sorely in need of a logical source of compassion so as to provide inspiration enabling finite beings to know the infinite. Although he speaks of compassion, it is only in a vague reference to an abstract attribute. The idea of an entity possessing compassion is avoided by Bohm (although he almost admits the need). He retreats from this idea because the standard notions of a personal God are dualistic and thus undermine the sense that reality at the most fundamental plane is unified.

Bohm's idea that the parts of the implicate order actually include the whole is not fully supported by his physical examples alone. Indeed, this is impossible to demonstrate mathematically. The part of the hologram is not *fully* representative of the whole. The part suffers from lack of resolution. It is qualitatively one but quantitatively different.

Bohm's explanation for the corruption in human society is another shortcoming in his theory. The theory alleges that evil arises from the explicate order. This is in contradiction with the basis of the theory, which states that everything in the explicate order unfolds from the implicate order. This means that evil and human society, or something at least resembling them, must be originally present in the implicate order. But what would lead us to believe that an undifferentiated entity would store anything even remotely resembling human society? How could there be evil in the implicate order if it is the source of love and compassion?

These are some of the scientific and philosophical problems with the theory of the implicate order pointed out by Thompson. These problems are resolved by Thompson, however, by replacing *advaita-vedānta* with *acintya-bhedābheda*. Simply stated, *acintya-bhedābheda* means that reality is inconceivably one and different at the same time. *Acintya-bhedābheda* holds that the world of material variety is illusory but not altogether false. It insists that there is a transcendental variety and spiritual individuality that lies beyond illusion.

The history of philosophy bears evidence that neither the concepts of oneness (nondualism) or difference (dualism) are adequate to fully describe the nature of being. Exclusive emphasis on oneness leads to the denial of the world and our very sense of self as an individual—viewing them as illusion. Exclusive emphasis on difference divides reality, creating an unbridgeable gap between man and God. Yet both concepts are essential inasmuch as unity is a necessary demand of our reason, while difference is an undeniable fact of our experience. A synthesis of the two can be seen as the goal of philosophy. In the theory of *acintya-bhedābheda,* the concepts of oneness and difference are transcended and reconciled into a higher synthesis; thus, they become complementary aspects of Godhead, for whom all things are possible.

The word *acintya* is central to the theory. It can be defined as the power to reconcile the impossible. *Acintya* is that which is inconceivable, because it involves contradictory notions, yet it can be appreciated through logical implication.

Acintya, inconceivable, is different from *anirvacanīya,* or indescribable, which is said to be the nature of transcendence in the monistic school of thought.[1] *Anirvacanīya* is the joining of the opposing concepts of reality and illusion, producing a canceling effect—a negative effect. *Acintya,* on the other hand, signifies a marriage of opposite concepts leading to a more complete unity—a positive effect.

1. Kapoor, O. B. L. *Philosophy and Religion of Śrī Chaitanya* (New Delhi, India: Munshiram Manoharlal, 1977), p. 157.

An example drawn from material nature may help us understand the concept of *acintya-bhedābheda.* We cannot think of fire without the power of burning; similarly, we cannot think of the power of burning without fire. Both are identical. While fire is nothing but that which burns; the power of burning is but fire in action. Fire and its burning power are not absolutely the same, however. If they were absolutely the same, there would be no need to warn children that fire burns. It would be sufficient to say "fire." In reality, the fire is the energetic source of the power to burn. From this example drawn from the world of our experience, we can deduce that the principle of simultaneous oneness and difference is all-pervading, appearing even in material objects.

Just as there is neither absolute oneness nor absolute difference in the material example of fire and burning power, there is neither absolute oneness nor absolute difference between Godhead and his energies. Godhead consists of both the energetic and the energy, which are one yet different. Godhead is complete without his various emanations. This is absolute completeness. No matter how much energy he distributes, he remains the complete balance.

In the theory of *acintya-bhedābheda,* the personal form of God exists beyond material time in a transtemporal state, where eternality and the passage of time are harmonized by the principle of simultaneous oneness and variegatedness. This principle also applies to transcendental form. In the material conception of form, the whole can be reduced to a mere juxtaposition of the parts. This makes the form secondary. In the theory of *acintya-bhedābheda,* the material conception of form is transcended. The Supreme Being is fully present in all the parts that make up the total reality and thus is one unified principle underlying all variegated manifestations. Yet he has his own personality and is different from his parts or energies at the same time. Each of the parts of Godhead's form are equal to each other and to the whole form as well. At the same time, each of the parts remains a part. This is fundamental to the philosophical outlook of *acintya-bhedābheda.* It allows for the eternal individuality of all things without the loss of oneness or harmony. It also allows for the possibility that human beings, even while possessing limited mind and senses, can come to know about the nature of transcendence. The infinite, being so, can and does reveal himself to the finite. Just as the eye cannot see the mind but can be in connection with it if the mind chooses to think about it, the finite can know about the infinite by the grace of the infinite.

If Godhead has personal form, it is reasonable to conclude that a transcendental society exists that resembles human society and could unfold as the explicate order. In this conception, the explicate order is a perverted reflection of the ultimate reality existing in the transcendental realm. The reflection of that realm, appearing as the explicate order, is the kingdom of God without God. It is without God inasmuch as God, being the center of the ultimate reality, no longer appears to be the center. This produces illusion and thus corruption. The basis of corruption is the misplaced sense of proprietorship resulting in the utterly false notions of "I" and "mine."

According to *acintya-bhedābheda,* the individual self is a minute particle of will or consciousness—a sentient being—endowed with a serving tendency. This tendency for service is a result of the individual self's dependency on the Supreme Self. The Supreme Self is the maintainer, while the individual self is maintained. This minute self is transcendental to matter and *qualitatively one* with Godhead while *quantitatively different.* The inherent smallness of the atomic soul in contrast to Godhead makes the atomic soul prone to illusion, whereas Godhead is not. This is analogous to the example of the hologram in which only a portion of the holographic plate is illuminated. The resultant image, although apparently complete, is slightly fuzzy and does not give the total three-dimensional view from all directions that one would observe if the entire holographic plate were illuminated.

Living in illusion, the atomic soul sees herself as separate from Godhead. As a result of imperfect sense perception, she makes false distinctions, such as good and bad, happy and sad. The minute self can also live in an enlightened state in complete harmony with the Godhead by the latter's grace—which is attracted by sincere petition or devotion. This is so because while independent and unlimited, Godhead is affectionately disposed to the atomic souls. The very nature of devotion is that it is of another world, and for it to be devotion in the full sense, it must be engaged in for its own sake and nothing else. This act of devotion is the purified function of the inherent serving tendency of the self. It makes possible a communion with Godhead. In this communion, the self becomes one *in purpose* with Godhead and eternally serves Godhead with no sense of separateness from him. If we accept this theory, there is scope for action from within the explicate order, such as prayer or meditation, to have influence upon the whole. At least it appears as though the atomic soul can have influence on the whole, although in reality the inspiration for prayer and meditation comes from Godhead.

Acintya-bhedābheda cannot be fully appreciated without reference to the Vedic literature, or revealed scripture. The truth of the personality of Godhead, a supreme controller and enjoyer, will never be demonstrated in the laboratory of the controlled experiment. We can only control that which is inferior to ourselves. Revealed scripture is one of the principal means through which Godhead chooses to make himself known to us. While we can explain Śrī Chaitanya's theory of *acintya-bhedābheda* and conception of a divine person to some extent in the language of logic and modern science, a more comprehensive understanding of his truth is derived from the essence of the revealed scripture.

5

THE BHĀGAVATA

The Vedic evidence is vast. It is the most voluminous body of literature on earth. It contains both spiritual and material knowledge and is written by divinely empowered sages. It was compiled by Vyāsadeva, who was instructed to do so by his spiritual master, Nārada Muni. This system in which the guru instructs his or her disciple in the dissemination of spiritual truth is called the paramparā *system of descending knowledge.*

The empirical, or ascending, approach to understanding the mystery of life is different from the *paramparā* system. The empirical approach is based upon three steps: 1) hypothesis, 2) experimentation and observation, and 3) theory or conclusion, more often called "fact." Vedic spiritual science, on the other hand, uses three proofs, or *pramāṇas,* two of which cover entirely the ground encompassed by the empirical scientific method. This leaves a third type of evidence at the disposal of the Vedic scientists, giving them a decisive edge over their Western counterparts. This third means of acquiring knowledge takes us to the heart of the difference between these two approaches.

The first limb of the Vedic way of arriving at truth is *pratyakṣa,* or direct sense perception, including the observations of others. The second limb is *anumāna,* or logical inference. The last and most important limb is *śabda pramāṇa,* or hearing from authoritative sources, such as revealed scripture and saints. Objective criteria for recognizing saints is found within the scriptures.

The Vedic evidence is *śabda pramāṇa,* or evidence through revelation in divine sound. Other types of *pramāṇa,* or evidence (direct sense perception and reasoning), will never bring us to a conclusive understanding of the absolute truth in and of themselves; they must be guided by *śabda.* Evidence derived through sense perception is faulty because the senses are imperfect. Evidence derived through the senses of others is similarly defective. *Anumāna,* reasoning or inference, is also incomplete, *tarkapratiṣṭhānāt.* The *Vedānta-sūtras* tell us that through *tarka* (argumentative mental conjecture) we will never get anywhere, *apratiṣṭhā.* One may know through inference that where there is smoke, there is fire, yet one may not know that before seeing the smoke from a distance, rain put out the fire. Furthermore, the argumentative, self-asserting disposition repels Godhead. For every logical argument there is a logical counter argument. Therefore, only divine revelation descending from the plane of the soul, the conscious world, has the power to disentangle the atomic soul from the material coverings—physical, mental, and intellectual.

When we try to solve a mystery, we have to present evidence to make our case. It is very difficult to make a conclusive case by piecing together clues; however, if we can find a credible eyewitness, his or her evidence is conclusive. Similarly, in trying to solve the mystery of life, the evidence gathered through direct sense perception, as well as that derived from logical conjecture, is inconclusive. Our direct sense perception, although an eyewitness account, is prejudiced by our association with material nature. We are seeing through the covering of material nature. We are like witnesses under the influence of the person we are testifying about. Conjecture based on evidence presented by a biased witness cannot be taken seriously. Thus sense perception and reasoning are both inconclusive means of knowing. However, evidence derived from the *ṛṣis* (seers) who composed the Vedic literature is conclusive. It is said that the Vedic wisdom existed before creation. It is the very knowledge of how the world works. Such knowledge exists, and out of it the world comes into being. The world does not arise from nothing, a void. The potent knowledge, which science only partially reveals, underlies the creation. If we understand this mystic knowledge fully through *śabda pramāṇa,* we can solve the mystery of life.

The Vedic wisdom is written for our times. The seers who wrote the *Vedas* viewed the world from a different vantage point than ours. They addressed the greatest need of human society. Just as there is an arrangement in nature to provide the necessities of the lower life forms, so there is an arrangement to meet the necessity of human society. The human necessity is to know not just how but, more importantly, why. Vedic knowledge is nature's provision to answer this question definitively.

If there is any conceptual framework to modern science from which its successes arise, it is the simplistic idea that all life is reducible to biochemical and ultimately molecular processes. The transcendentalists, however, accept a hierarchical structure of realities culminating in the divine. Although the scientific view is well-formed, it has come about as a result of experimentation; therefore, it does not rest on a secure foundation, but formulates concepts based on conjecture derived from ongoing experimentation. While the transcendentalist works from a broad base down to specifics, modern science collects data from the world and then tries to draw conclusions about the nature of truth—a clearly speculative and thus inferior approach.

The problem with the modern scientific approach is twofold: one, a view based solely on experimentally derived data is subject to change when new and even contradictory data arises through subsequent experimentation. This unstable structure can totter at any time, and thus it would be difficult to build a stable society upon it. For example, entire schools of medical education and funding for medical projects would be risky ventures, because everything could change if conflicting verifiable data arises. Although it seems laudable theoretically to experiment, go forward, and be prepared to change direction at any time, it is highly impractical on a societal level. This brings us to the second problem, which is that consistent data does arise regularly, challenging the existing paradigm. But due to the fact that there is so much at stake, it is often ignored, or experimentation loses its objectivity inasmuch as it accepts only data that conforms with the existing worldview. In other words, speculation, which modern science is seeded in, invariably lends to loss of integrity. Ironically, modern science is often billed as the noble pursuit of truth.

Experimentation is a valid means of acquiring relative knowledge, but in order that it not degenerate into self-deception, it must be conducted within a larger framework that includes descending knowledge. The unbiased must ask themselves, "Is there perfect knowledge?" If the answer is "no," we may as well stop there. But Western thinking assumes that there is perfect knowledge to which we can evolve. However, the questionable means of evolution involves the utilization of imperfect instruments and human frailties. Vedic science also admits to perfect knowledge, but being that it is perfect, that knowledge is considered superior to humanity, and thus human society can attain it only if it chooses to reveal itself. Perfect knowledge has an agenda of its own!

The Vedic evidence consists of the four *Vedas: Ṛg, Sāma, Atharva, and Yajur*. In them, knowledge of medicine, military arts, astronomy, astrology, and many other material sciences are explained. From the *Vedas* comes the *Upaniṣads,* of which there are 108 principal books. The *Upaniṣads* deal more directly with transcendence, yet they do so indirectly by explaining that which we are not. The *Vedas* and the *Upaniṣads* are considered *śruti,* that which is heard directly from the speaking of the Lord. The balance of the Vedic literature consisting primarily of the *Purāṇas, Itihāsas,* and the six *vedāṅgas* is called *smṛti,* that which is remembered after having heard (the *śruti).* Of the two, the *smṛti* is more important. It is referred to as the "fifth *Veda."*

The importance of the *smṛti* is overlooked by certain scholars, and this results in a distortion of the Vedic evidence. Such misinformed persons, while extolling the *śruti,* fail to examine it thoroughly. The *śruti* sings the virtues of the *smṛti,* and the *smṛti* echoes the same. Thus, the *smṛti* further confirms that its content is but the elaboration of the essence of the *śruti.* One of the most important followers of Śrī Chaitanya, Śrī Jīva Goswāmī, has made a strong case for the importance of the *smṛti,* and ultimately the *Bhāgavata,* in his thesis, *Tattva Sandarbha.* Jīva Goswāmī has drawn many references from the vast body of Vedic literature to establish his point. In the *Mādhyandina-śruti* we find, "The *Ṛg, Yajur, Sāma,* and *Atharva Vedas,* as well as the *Itihāsas* and the *Purāṇas,* are the breath of Godhead." *Chāndogya Upaniṣad* further confirms, *itihāsaṁ purāṇaṁ pañcamaṁ vedānāṁ vedaṁ.* "The *Purāṇas* and *Itihāsas* are the fifth *Veda."* The *smṛti* amplifies this truth. In the *Vāyu Purāṇa* we find, "The *Purāṇas* are parts of the original *Yajur Veda."* The *Viṣṇu Purāṇa* further states, "The purports of all the *Vedas* are contained within the *Purāṇas* and *Itihāsas."* In the *Nārada Purāṇa,* Śiva advises his consort Pārvatī, "I consider that the *Purāṇas* are superior to the *Vedas.* . . . Anyone who has a different opinion is cursed to take birth as an animal." Jīva Goswāmī has offered many other references to establish the importance of the *smṛti.* These references are necessary if we are to consider the *Bhāgavata* with proper regard.

If the *smṛti* is more important than the *śruti*, one might ask, What is the most important part of the *smṛti?* The answer is the *Purāṇas*, and within the *Purāṇas* the *Bhāgavata.* In the *Prabhāsa-khaṇḍa* of the *Skānda Purāṇa*, it is mentioned, *yan na dṛṣṭam hi vedeṣu. . . . tat purāṇaiḥ pragīyate.* "[The confidential] truths not revealed in the *Vedas* are described in the *Purāṇas.* One who is fully conversant with the four *Vedas*, the six *vedāṅgas*, and the *Upaniṣads*, but who has not also studied the *Purāṇas*, is not actually learned in Vedic knowledge." The *Purāṇas* are presented in a literary style that makes the truth of the Vedas readily accessible in this age. Inasmuch as people in our times are fond of learning a lesson through the narration of a story, and a lesson is better learned when presented in such a format, the *Purāṇas* are Vedic wisdom tailored for our times. That the Bhāgavata is the essence of the *purāṇic* wisdom is no secret to those familiar with the *smṛti.*

To establish the *Bhāgavata* as the scripture par excellence, Jīva Goswāmī refers back to the *Vedānta-sūtras.* As mentioned earlier, a *sampradāya*, or spiritual tradition, that has no commentary on the *Vedānta-sūtras* is considered useless by those acquainted with Vedic knowledge. This is so because these *sūtras* were written as an explanation of the *Vedas* and *Purāṇas* by the author, Vyāsadeva, himself. The *sūtras* are a guide to understanding the Vedic literature, without which it is impossible to know the import of Vedic wisdom. Yet because these *sūtras* are coded aphorisms, their meaning is the subject of considerable debate. It is the opinion of Jīva Goswāmī that Vyāsadeva wrote the *Bhāgavata* as a natural commentary on the *sūtras*, revealing in plain language the inner meaning of the *Vedas.* The *smṛti* corroborates this conclusion, as does the *Bhāgavata* itself.

The *Bhāgavata* begins by invoking the *gāyatrī mantra (dhīmahi).* This indicates that the *Bhāgavata* is an explanation of the *gāyatrī mantra,* as confirmed in the *Garuḍa Purāṇa: gāyatrī bhāṣya rūpo 'sau vedārtha paribṛṁhitaḥ.* Because the *gāyatrī mantra* is famous, mention of the word *dhīmahi* in the first verse of the *Bhāgavata* is sufficient to indicate that the entire *mantra* is being invoked. The *gāyatrī mantra* is the essence of all Vedic knowledge. It was first delivered to Brahmā by Śrī Kṛṣṇa through his flute. When the flute sound of the *gāyatrī mantra* entered the heart of Brahmā, he expanded his impression as the Vedic wisdom and, subsequently, the entire creation by sound *(śabda).* Thus the *gāyatrī mantra* is the mother of the Vedas. The *Bhāgavata,* as an explanation of the *gāyatrī mantra,* is the essence of the Vedic wisdom.

The *Bhāgavata* was compiled after Vyāsa completed every other Vedic text. The *Bhāgavata* describes that Vyāsa felt despondent, even after compiling all the Vedic knowledge for the benefit of the world. With the help of Nārada Muni, his spiritual master, he realized the cause of his despondency was that he had not directly emphasized the whole truth. Rather, catering to the conditioning of the living entities ensnared in illusion, he described, in a roundabout fashion, the nature of truth. This indirect approach lends itself to various interpretations of "truth," all of which may be half-truths at best. Yet there is a need to present the truth indirectly, for otherwise it may not be listened to at all. Just as a child may not take medicine unless it is sugarcoated, people do not have a taste for the truth, even though it is the medicine they so need. Thus compiling the Vedic knowledge into so many texts was necessary. Yet without directly stating the truth, the task was incomplete. Thus Nārada Muni chastised Vyāsa for misleading the people and pointed out the need for the *Bhāgavata.*

The *Garuḍa, Matsya, Skānda,* and *Nārada Purāṇas* all glorify the *Bhāgavata.* All of the Vaiṣṇava commentaries on the *Vedānta-sūtras* are supported by way of reference to the *Bhāgavata*. Although Śaṅkara did not touch the *Bhāgavata*, his successors could not ignore it in their attempt to propagate their *advaita-vedānta* philosophy. Thus many monists have tried awkwardly to harmonize it with their doctrine of nonduality. Da Free John, for example, considers the *Bhāgavata* the literary essence of what he refers to as "The Great Tradition" and attempts to establish his quasi-devotional monism with it. The *Bhāgavata* consists of almost eighteen thousand verses in twelve cantos. The essence of the *Bhāgavata* is found in the five chapters describing the *rasa* dance. Yet the reader is cautioned not to jump to these chapters, for the entire *Bhāgavata* must be read so that its essence not be misinterpreted. From the *Bhāgavata* (SB 1.7.4), we learn *apaśyat puruṣaṁ pūrṇaṁ māyāṁ ca tad-apāśrayam:* Vyāsa had a vision of the Lord and the world of illusion. He saw the remedial measure for all suffering, and particularly for this age (Kali-yuga), to be *bhakti-yogam adhokṣaje* (devotion to Godhead). Thus Vyāsa conceived of the *Bhāgavata* in spiritual trance. Then he wrote notes on his conception, which became known as the *Vedānta-sūtras.* After writing the *Vedānta-sūtras,* he fully explained the *sūtras* in the form of the *Bhāgavata* for the benefit of the entire world.

The *Bhāgavata* is more than a book, more even than a scripture. It is the ripened fruit of the desire tree of Vedic literature. The desire tree of Vedic literature yields all knowledge. Its ripened fruit is the end of knowledge, love absolute. The *Bhāgavata* rejects anything short of this ideal: *dharmaḥ projjhita-kaitavo 'tra.* (SB 1.1.2) What is the end of knowledge, the truth of love? This is where the *Bhāgavata* surpasses all other books, for it speaks directly about that which other scriptures only point in the direction of. A book only indicates that which it describes, just as a watch is an indicator of time. We may tell the time by glancing at our watch, but we have not captured time by purchasing a wristwatch. Similarly, the scripture is only an indicator. Yet if we took the experience of life and distilled it to its essence, the elixir derived would point us in the direction of the essence of the *Bhāgavata*. If this world is a reflection of reality, the shadow of the substance, through the reflection we should be able to arrive at an understanding of the nature of the truth. If we read the *Bhāgavata* carefully, we will be able to see correctly that which is already before our eyes.

It is significant that the *Bhāgavata* mentions two types of "*Bhāgavata*"—the book *Bhāgavata* and the person *Bhāgavata*. If the book *Bhāgavata* has any limitations, it is only in the sense that it is a passive agent of divinity, whereas the personification of the book, the person *Bhāgavata,* is the active agent of divinity. An active agent of divinity brings the book to life. From such a person we can learn to appreciate the book *Bhāgavata,* as the book walks among us laden with the fruits of love.

The purport of the book *Bhāgavata* is to follow the person *Bhāgavata*. Spiritual life is not an intellectual exercise. Neither is it a physical or mental exercise. It is the Absolute exercising itself in relation to the finite, initiating the jīva soul's spiritual journey. The *Bhāgavata,* while addressing our intellect, does so such that we conclusively understand the shortcoming of intellectual pursuit. Readers of the *Bhāgavata* undergo a bashing of their intellect. The *Bhāgavata* is intended for those afflicted with the hankering for scholarship. If such persons study the *Bhāgavata* under the guidance of a saint, this punitive but remedial measure will cure them of their addiction to intellectual gymnastics, which is always an inconclusive way of knowing.

The *Bhāgavata* is written in Sanskrit, but we would be wrong to conclude that knowing Sanskrit is a prerequisite to understanding the *Bhāgavata*. Sanskrit is a product of the deluding potency of Godhead, *viṣṇu-māyā*. It cannot reveal the absolute truth. The revealed scripture tells us that through the preceptorial lineage alone, by submission to the saints, we can know the truth.

The mundane intellect is one part of the composite of the subtle material body, which encases the *jīva* soul. The intellect is greater than the mind and body, yet lesser than the soul and Godhead. If we try to understand Godhead but are unwilling to pass beyond the physical realm, we will know only the shadow of God, the material world. The *Bhāgavata* rejects the materialistic approach, calling it *kaitava-dharma*, cheating religion or imitation. Similarly, if we try to know Godhead through the intellect, we will turn into atheists or monists.

Although monists attempt to close down the senses, mind, and intellect, inhibition of mental activity through intellectual, mental, and physical methods is itself a negative form of physical, mental, and intellectual activity. All intellectual, mental-emotional, and physical activity corresponds to the dormant state of the soul. The material nature is animated by consciousness; however, consciousness in association with material nature is asleep to its full potential. Thus, if we are interested in a wholly spiritual life, we must contact the world of consciousness, the spiritual world. If all variety, which is the spice of life in the material plane, amounts to the life of the sleeping soul, we can hardly conceive of how beautiful and engaging the world of the awakened soul is. The spiritual world is not a void, yet it escapes description. It can only be represented crudely by the artist's brush or the writer's pen. Yet what has been written about the spiritual world in the *Bhāgavata* is endearing and encouraging to our souls. The saints are the active agents of that realm. The scripture is the passive agent of the same. Scripture is the word of the *sādhu*, the saint, who acts as an instrument of Godhead.

The *sādhu*, bearing the message of Godhead, does the impossible. It is impossible for the finite soul to know the infinite Godhead. Even your own soul will not fit within the limits of your intellect, what to speak of fitting God within your intellect. If, however, the infinite Godhead chooses to make himself known to the finite, the finite soul transcends the land where impossible is a word in everyone's dictionary. The *sādhu* is the agent through whom Godhead chooses, out of his infinite capacity, to reveal himself to the finite. If he could not do so, he would not be truly infinite.

Many of Śrī Chaitanya's followers were intellectual giants. They wrote many books in the most sophisticated philosophical language. Yet they did so on the order of Śrī Chaitanya, who thus used their intellects in the service of Godhead. This is an instance of the Godhead engaging the atomic soul, and the atomic soul engaging his or her intellect in the service of Godhead. This is worlds apart from insisting that Godhead submit to our intellect. The intellect can only be the guide of the soul to a point. While it can help us rise above a life of mental and sensual demands, it cannot reveal the fullness of the soul or the truth about the personality of Godhead. Revealing this truth is the prerogative of Godhead, who chooses to do so in the form of the Bhāgavata, both book and person. In the very least, Śrī Chaitanya is such a person, appearing to teach us by example this important principle.

Śrī Chaitanya and his followers have accepted the *Bhāgavata* "as it is." They saw no need for a separate commentary on the *Vedānta-sūtras*, yet later, for the sake of establishing themselves in the eyes of the other lineages, a commentary was written by Baladeva Vidyābhūṣaṇa. This commentary, *Govinda-bhāṣya,* surpasses all the preceding commentaries in excellence, thus ornamenting the lineage of Śrī Chaitanya. The *Bhāgavata* is the scriptural basis for Śrī Chaitanya's doctrine of divine love. From the *Bhāgavata,* Śrī Chaitanya establishes that transcendence is suprasensual, supraemotional, and ultimately suprasexual.

As mentioned, both Rāmānuja and Madhva drew upon the *Bhāgavata* in writing their respective commentaries on the *Vedānta-sūtras.* Yet while Śrī Chaitanya's God of inconceivable, simultaneous oneness and difference is Rādhā-Kṛṣṇa, Rāmānuja places greater emphasis on Viṣṇu, while Madhva only partially describes Kṛṣṇa. In doing so they miss the full purport of the *Bhāgavata.* Viṣṇu is no doubt God, but in Śrī Chaitanya's vision, Kṛṣṇa is beyond God, and greater still is devotion to Kṛṣṇa, which is most completely personified as Śrī Rādhā, his feminine counterwhole.

6

VAIDHI-BHAKTI AND THE VIṢṆU OF VAIKUṆṬHA

Viṣṇu of Vaikuṇṭha is very different from the God of Christianity, at least in appearance. Yet there are also similarities between the two. Viṣṇu is a just God, although his love and mercy are more prominent. Like God the Father, he is seated on a jeweled throne, majestic, almighty, and surrounded by unimaginable opulence. He is otherworldly, living in a transcendental domain where the streets are paved with gold. Concerning Christianity's blackout on the details of God's personal characteristics and appearance, the personhood of Viṣṇu sheds some light, thus lending necessary support to the strongest point of Western religious tradition—the concept of a personal God.

Viṣṇu is not limited by time and space. He exists everywhere at all times. When we think of God as a person, we tend naturally to think of him from within our frame of reference. But it is our limited frame of reference that God seeks to free us from. It is not difficult for God to do so, but it requires our willingness, for love is voluntary. Thus Godhead wants the living entities to want to love him. And to love him is to not love the world as perceived by the five senses and the mind, a misperception in which we mistakenly see ourselves rather than Godhead as the center.

Viṣṇu of *Vaikuṇṭha* is an important qualifier, for there are various Viṣṇus described in the Vedic literature. Vaikuṇṭha Viṣṇu, also known as Narāyaṇa, is the fountainhead of all other partial expressions of himself. For example, the Viṣṇu of the triumvirate Brahmā, Viṣṇu, and Śiva is only a partial expression of the original Viṣṇu. Viṣṇu appears in many forms in order to accomplish various tasks, all of which can be summed up in the twofold purpose of giving joy to the godly and diminishing ungodly influences in the world.

Rāmānuja's Vaiṣṇavism does not allow for more than one God, but a God who has the capacity to appear in various forms. Although we are all parts of God, the sum of the parts does not equal the whole. Viṣṇu and his different incarnations can be compared to different versions of the same computer. For example, there are many versions of the Macintosh PowerBook computer, such as the PowerBook 145, the 160, and the 180. Just as these are all different grades of the same computer, yet each one is fully functional as a computer, similarly there are different incarnations of Viṣṇu—some of which are more transcendentally complete than others. Although we are parts and parcels of Godhead, we are different in constitution. We are not God, rather one of his energies. In computer language, we are like a small chip in any of the PowerBooks, not an independent computer. Thus there is a big difference between ourselves and God, even while there is considerable similarity.

Just as we have changes of dress for different engagements, and with these changes of dress varied expressions of our personality, so does Viṣṇu. At work one may be known as Mr. Jones, dressed in suit and tie. After work the same man is known by his first name by friends with whom he relaxes. His children know him as dad, and they see a particular side of their father. His wife knows him most intimately by still other names that no one else knows him by. She knows of all other aspects of her husband's personality and also aspects of his personality that no one else knows. This is an important point upon which I will elaborate in later chapters. For now, it is sufficient to consider that if we have different appearances and names, yet remain one person, certainly God can do the same.

Whereas we can be in only one place at a time, Viṣṇu appears in different places at the same time, performing varieties of pastimes. This is no doubt extraordinary, yet we also do this to some extent with the help of modern technology. Every evening Peter Jennings appears in millions of living rooms at the same time, keeping us up to date with the latest news of our world. If we can do this by manipulating the fire element (electricity), and with only limited understanding of this one element of material existence, surely Viṣṇu can do much more. He does, appearing in various incarnations bringing us news of the spiritual world.

A description of Viṣṇu's form and attributes is found in the *Bhāgavata.* Viṣṇu has four arms. His transcendental body is bluish. His forehead is adorned with *tilaka* and his body is decorated with ornaments and jewels. In his hands he holds four symbolic items: conch shell, club, disk *(sudarśana),* and lotus. On his chest he wears a jewel called *kaustubha,* and an imprint called *śrīvatsa.* The elements of his body are not bile, mucus, and air, as are our own. His body is *sat* (eternity), *cit* (cognizance), and *ānanda* (bliss). The material elements form an existence that is *asat* (temporal), *acit* (full of ignorance), and *nirānanda* (full of misery). The reversal of these material characteristics can logically form a world of eternity, knowledge, and bliss. Such a world is free from anxiety, Vaikuṇṭha. The *Bhāgavata* refers to this plane as *adhokṣaja,* that which is beyond our ability to grasp. It is unrivaled in majesty and is overtly spiritual in appearance. Only if Viṣṇu wants us to know of it can we experience that plane. Going there depends entirely upon his grace.

The basis of the spiritual world is service, which is the basis of love. We cannot separate service from love.

Exploitation is the basis of the material world. Here all service is tinged with exploitation. We serve for something other than service itself, such as for money, food, fame, or knowledge. Even if we give to the most philanthropic cause, we are not wholly selfless, for our service springs from a sense of the self and the world that is based on sense perception. What we see with our senses, and reason further about with our minds and the help of other's material experience, is not the whole picture. Philanthropy is an extended form of ego gratification that reaches beyond immediate bodily gratification and caters to the subtle form of our material condition, the mental system. The good feeling we get from feeding the poor, for example, is often one that caters to our mental conception of what the world is (as understood through the medium of the senses), a notion that is sure to be mistaken. It caters to our illusory conception of the self, sometimes leading to mistaking oneself to be the Savior, the Lord. It is a subtle form of self-centeredness. Service for its own sake can only be realized when we cease making a service agenda and serve the will of Godhead. This type of service is what Vaikuṇṭha is made of.

Viṣṇu is served in awe and reverence by pure souls who have spiritual bodies similar to the body of their Lord. The soul in material consciousness finds itself surrounded by a material body. The material body is an expression of the soul's consciousness in touch with material nature. Similarly, pure spiritual consciousness, when awakened in spiritual love, produces a spiritual body. That body is within the soul in potential, just as a tree lies in potential within the seed. Within the appropriate environment, just as the tree grows, so does the soul's spiritual form. This is the beginning of a real body-positive spirituality. It involves converting the material body into a spiritual body by the gradual spiritualization of one's consciousness. It is a soul-positive spirituality as well, because it does not deny the existence of individuality, as does monism. In Vaikuṇṭha, spiritual individuals endowed with love of Viṣṇu engage in reciprocal dealings with their Lord eternally. The duality of material existence is transcended, yet spiritual variety is manifest.

Nothing could be more obvious than the fact that all souls thrive on love. The soul's need for a meaningful and loving relationship, as expressed from within the material covering, is fulfilled when our loving propensity is reposed in Godhead, thus bringing the soul out from beneath the blanket of material slumber. The forms of loving exchange we are familiar with in the material sphere mirror the spiritual relationships that enlightened souls experience with Godhead. Of these relationships *(rasas)*, the relationship of servant and master is prominent in Vaikuṇṭha. While a sense of neutrality or equipoise *(śānta-rasa)* also dominates, loving service in awe and reverence *(dāsya-rasa)*, is the closest relationship the *jīvātmā* (atomic soul) can have with Viṣṇu.

The means to attain Vaikuṇṭha is the very devotion that Vaikuṇṭha is based on. Devotion is both the means and the goal. The *Bhāgavata* stresses pure devotion, both regulated and spontaneous. Outwardly, the *Bhāgavata* stresses regulated devotion, which is called *vaidhi-bhakti*. The impetus for *vaidhi-bhakti* is rules and regulations. Any genuine system of transcendental culture is based on a code of ethics. Pātanjali's yoga system begins with *yama-niyama*, which are rules and regulations. To practice yoga and begin with *āsanas*, as many people in the West do today, is to jump ahead in the eightfold system of yoga. The proper starting point involves having a worldview that is in concert with the yoga philosophy. For example, *ahiṁsā*, or nonviolence, is an ethical principle of the yogic worldview. Thus the yoga practitioner is expected to be vegetarian in diet. Because yoga is a system intended to help a practitioner realize that he or she is not the body or mind, abstinence from sex is recommended. Certainly unrestricted sex life takes one outside of the yogic foundation of *yama niyama.* Similarly, *vaidhi-bhakti,* or regulated devotion, is based on scriptural imperatives both positive and negative. Flawless execution of *vaidhi-bhakti* attracts the grace of Godhead, who delivers the aspiring soul to Vaikuṇṭha. The soul becomes free from the anxiety resulting from following the dictates of the material mind and senses by accepting the rules and regulations of Viṣṇu.

That God is a person is the solution to all of our problems, for in him we find a person whom we can serve and love, one who will not let us down. He is infallible, unlike every other person we know. But the fact that God is a person is also a problem for us, because to love him we have to learn to make his likes our likes and his dislikes our dislikes. This separates us from the misleading dictates of our imperfect senses. Making his likes our likes, and his dislikes our dislikes, is the beginning of a life of devotion. This does not repress the senses, but trains them to serve their master. A devotee accomplishes this by serving an established Deity of Viṣṇu in the temple. There are sixty-four different items of worship. In the temple setting, the devotees all follow the schedule of the Deity twenty-four hours a day. Among other things, the devotees bathe, dress, sing for, cook for, and hold festivals in honor of the Deity as if the temple was the spiritual world.

Before one can appreciate Deity worship, one has to overcome certain ideas about God bequeathed to us by those who may have been victims of misconception or misunderstanding. According to Dr. William Deadwyler, in his insightful article entitled "The Devotee and the Deity: Living a Personalistic Theology," "[Certain] ideas make it difficult for most Westerners to understand the divine image. Of course, there are the strong Old Testament proscriptions against idol worship, promulgated to keep the followers of Yahweh from bowing down before the Baals and Ishtars of their neighbors, but more significant for the classical Judeo-Christian idea of God is the later intellectual interpretation of divinity in terms of a negative theology derived from Greek speculative metaphysics, with its disdain for the particular and the sensual. This resulted in an understanding of God as a being who by His own intrinsic nature cannot possibly be concretely depicted."[1]

Gauḍīya Vaiṣṇava saint and theologian Bhaktivinode Ṭhākura speaks with finality in his charming style that overflows with realization: "Holy men to whom God has been pleased to show His spiritual form have often attempted to picture it to their fellow brethren. The picture, whether it be by pencil, chisel, or pen, is always made through the medium of matter, and hence a degree of grossness has all along attended the representations. This emblematic exhibition of spiritual impressions is far from being open to [the] charge of idolatry. Those who rationally conceive the idea of God, and by the assistance of the imagination create an image, are certainly open to the charge. There is one absolute truth at the bottom of this important question. It is this: Nature has indeed a relation to the spirit. What is that relation? As far as we have been instructed by the inner Tutor, we may safely say, that spirit is the perfect model and nature is the copy which is full of imperfections. Draw inferences

1. Deadwyler, William. "The Devotee and the Deity; Living a Personalistic Theology," *Gods of Flesh, Gods of Stone: The Embodiment of Divinity in India* (Chambersburg, PA: Anima Books, 1985)

from the side of nature and press them upon the Deity, they will ever remain gross and imperfect. Draw from the spirit inside and push your impressions at first to the mind and then to the body, you simply spiritualize them both. Here is [the] advent of God on the scene of nature. . . . The spiritual form thus conveyed to us is none but the eternal form of God. The grossness is simply apparent, but all the actions and consequences are fully spiritual. . . . Here we find the absolute in the relative, the positive in the negative and spirit in matter. The spiritual form of God is therefore an eternal truth and with all its inward variety, it is one Undivided Unity. What appears to be a contradiction to reason is nothing but the rule of spirit, and the greatest surprise arises when we see full harmony in all these contradictions."[2]

Śaṅkara's monists argue that God is beyond form. They say that God is unlimited and thus cannot be confined to form. But those who believe that God is impersonal often identify him with a power or attribute of nature, though in fact he is above nature and all her laws. It is sacrilegious to confine God by identifying him with attributes that exist only within time and space. His excellence lies in having mutually contradicting powers and attributes ruled by his superhuman self. Thus he possesses a form that is free from material limitations and is beyond time and space.

It does not suffice to say that the forms of our ordinary experience, our material bodies and other material forms, are the forms of Godhead. Neither can we say that the world itself is the form of God and leave it at that. Although all of these forms certainly have a connection with Godhead, they are bound by time and space. They are but an energy or particular potency of Godhead *(māyā-śakti)*, not

2. Rupavilasa Dasa. *The Seventh Goswami* (Washington, MS: New Jaipur Press, 1989), pp. 155–156.

the energetic source. The source also has form and his form is transcendental. According to Vaiṣṇava philosophy, Godhead has many forms, each issuing from the original form, each of which are partial expressions of his divine personality.

In addition, all the great scriptures of the world instruct us to love God, not merely to know him. How can we love something formless or void? We are all persons, and we desire to love other persons. We desire personal relationships, and the ultimate relationship is with the personhood of the Godhead. The undifferentiated spiritual light known by the Hindus as the *Brahman* is certainly an awe-inspiring concept. It is something we can appreciate, but hardly love. *Brahman* consciousness is the plane of pure knowledge—not the plane of love, beauty, and ecstasy.

Devotion to Viṣṇu in his plane of love is not an artificial imposition. After all, devotion, or service, is the natural characteristic of the soul. All souls are serving at all times. We serve our family, our planet, and our mind's demands. The *dharma* of the soul is to serve. We cannot separate service from the individual unit of consciousness any more than we can separate wetness from water. We are all consciousness, but taking a closer look at the nature of consciousness, we can conclude that it is dedicating in nature. Our predicament is that we do not know where to repose our dedicating nature such that we will find fulfillment. The true center for all devotion is Viṣṇu, because he has the capacity to reciprocate for every ounce of service. When our serving tendency is improperly reposed in Viṣṇu's material energy *(māyā-śakti)*, our identity as units of service is obscured. This is called illusion. While Godhead is the actual knower and owner of all things, he who is to be served by all beings, in illusion we think ourselves as masters and try to own and know as much as we can rather than serve he who knows all and owns all. By such service nothing remains to be known or possessed, for Godhead, who is conquered by love, becomes the possession of the devotee.

God is the center and we are on the circumference. There can only be one God, one center, if we are to have harmony. But all souls conceive of themselves as the center, based on a perception of the world derived from the senses and mind. It is our world of black and white, good and bad, happy and sad. It is our reality, but it is not the Absolute Truth. When each individual unit of consciousness thinks herself to be the center, there is no hope for peace. There can be unlimited servants, but only one God. In material consciousness we think the more servants we have, the better our position will be. Spiritual life, on the other hand, is all about serving. Thus if we can surround ourselves with those who are more spiritually advanced, our position is that much enhanced. Serve we must, and to serve those who serve God is best.

Service to Viṣṇu in regulated devotion, however, is not the full picture of devotion advocated in the *Bhāgavata.* Regulated service is devotion that lacks spontaneity. It involves some calculation. The inhabitants of Vaikuṇṭha serve with the knowledge that Viṣṇu is God and thus he ought to be served. This serving disposition, while pure and transcendental, is nonetheless service that forms only the basis of love. If we love someone, we serve him or her. But there is further development in love that is only hinted at in Vaikuṇṭha. Viṣṇu has other more intimate dealings with his immediate associates, dealings that we cannot directly enter into. Viṣṇu, for example, is not asexual. He has a wife, Lakṣmī.

Viṣṇu is the *śaktiman* and Lakṣmī is the *śakti*—the potent and the potency. The Lord is *puruṣa,* the enjoyer, and Lakṣmī is *prakṛti,* the enjoyed. Both are interdependent aspects of divinity. One compliments the other. Although an abstract principle, *prakṛti* is personified as Lakṣmī. She is the perfect wife in the classical sense: she never leaves her husband's side. She is the Goddess of fortune, who is always with Viṣṇu. But the *Bhāgavata* makes mention of Lakṣmī's desire to associate with Kṛṣṇa in his *rasa* dance. Thus the very bible of devotion, the *Bhāgavata,* leads us to the land of spontaneous devotion—Vṛndāvana, the land of Kṛṣṇa. Kṛṣṇa is the transcendental Cupid, whom Viṣṇu is only a partial expression of. The feminine aspect of divinity, *śakti,* plays a very important part in Śrī Chaitanya's Vaiṣṇava philosophy. Understanding more completely the influence of the feminine aspect of divinity is crucial to our arrival at a sexually pure and positive spirituality. For this, we will have to go beyond Vaikuṇṭha and the Viṣṇu of Rāmānuja to the teaching of Śrī Chaitanya. For Rāmānuja, Viṣṇu's *śakti,* Lakṣmī, is of secondary importance. For Śrī Chaitanya, this *śakti* in her highest expression, Śrī Rādhā, is the pure transcendental expression of sexuality *(hlādinī-śakti)* and the last word in spirituality.

7

Śrī Chaitanya and the Path of Spontaneous Devotion

Spontaneity is the full face of devotion. Thus when we are advised to regulate it, we hesitate. We want to move freely and naturally, unconstrained by rules and regulations. We may want to serve God spontaneously without conforming to any religious dogma. But who is God? What does God want? These are important questions. Knowledge is required in order that our "service" is not disservice. If a child is crying, we may want to comfort her. But if we give her milk without knowing that the cause of her discomfort is too much gas in her stomach, we render a disservice.

Devotion we have, but it is flowing in the wrong direction due to the ignorance of bodily identification. Our devotion flows spontaneously in the direction of the ocean of sense indulgence. We so identify with our material body that if it calls upon us, without thinking, we are there. Thus regulating our contaminated spontaneity is necessary that its polluted stream might become pure and flow unchecked into the ocean of pure devotion. Once our raga, or spontaneity, is healthy, the need for regulation recedes into the background.

Regulation and spontaneity are not opposed to one another. In the school of Śrī Chaitanya, regulation ultimately promotes spontaneous devotion to Kṛṣṇa, the Deity of this lineage. While Śrī Chaitanya's followers worship the Deity of Kṛṣṇa much like other devotees worship Viṣṇu, their goal is somewhat different. The aim of Śrī Chaitanya's followers is developing intimacy with Godhead beyond awe and reverence. The *sādhana* (spiritual practice) in this lineage develops gradually beyond the jurisdiction of rules and regulations to spontaneous devotion. In this stage of *sādhana* the devotee cultivates a spiritual disposition, following in the footsteps of one of Śrī Kṛṣṇa's eternal associates in Vṛndāvana. In this way the devotees prepare themselves for eventually entering into the pastimes of Kṛṣṇa, either as a servant of Kṛṣṇa, a friend, an elder well-wisher, or in the optimum a lover. This path of spontaneous devotion, articulated by Śrī Chaitanya, is the highest reading of the *Bhāgavata.*

Śrī Chaitanya embraced the *Bhāgavata* as no other *ācārya* has, with both arms drawing it close to his heart. It is said that one of his closest followers, Gadādhara, used to read the *Bhāgavata* to him daily when he resided in Jagannātha Purī, a holy place *(tīrtha)* on the eastern coast of India. Yet their reading was frustrated by the incessant tears of joy that flowed from their eyes, wetting the pages of the manuscript. To his followers, Śrī Chaitanya is the personification of the *Bhāgavata.* He is Kṛṣṇa, the subject of the *Bhāgavata,* yet moreover he is Kṛṣṇa in the mood of his principal *śakti,* Śrī Rādhā, who alone can fully satisfy the personality of Godhead as his counterwhole.

These are indeed esoteric concepts that require considerable explanation. Such explanations can help us conceptualize the spiritual source of our innate drive for relationship. They solve the mystery of eros, leaving it to us to embrace the solution. Yet before diving deeply within the ocean of *bhakti-rasa* (the mellows of devotion), an account of the exoteric side of Śrī Chaitanya's life will help us appreciate the esoteric truth of his appearance and find hope in our search for love.

Śrī Chaitanya appeared in this world in 1486 in the district of Nadia, Navadvīpa, West Bengal on the stellar occasion of a full lunar eclipse. Thousands of Hindus were bathing in the Ganges River and chanting the names of God at the time in order to counteract the apparently inauspicious astrological influence. Neighboring Muslims chanted as well, mocking the Hindu constituency of Muslim-ruled Bengal. Śrī Chaitanya's appearance was thus most auspicious, converting an inauspicious stellar influence into a time of divine contemplation.

His parents, Jagannātha Miśra and Śacīdevī, were of brāhmaṇa lineage. They named their son Viśvambhara, which means he who maintains the world. It was customary at the time to name one's son or daughter after God, conceiving of the child as a servant of divinity. Yet the significance of their newborn son's appearance was extraordinary and the name quite befitting.

The early life of Śrī Chaitanya was filled with indications of his divinity. Even though he chose not to unveil the purpose of his descent in his childhood, the truth of his divinity invariably came to the surface. When as an infant he would cry, only the chanting of the names of God by his elders could cause him to stop. As a youth he engaged in endless scholarship, becoming not only the best student in his class, but the greatest scholar of his time. At sixteen he defeated the renowned Keśava Kāśmiri, who bore the distinguished title of *digvijaya* (one who has conquered all other pundits). The pundit was a devotee of the Goddess of learning, Saraswatī. Astounded by his defeat at the hands of a mere student of grammar, the pundit petitioned the Goddess as to the cause of her devotee's embarrassment. In a dream the Goddess informed him that she considered herself a devotee of this boy of Nadia. Eventually Keśava Kāśmiri became Śrī Chaitanya's disciple.

Śrī Chaitanya played with knowledge as if it were clay, molding it into arguments and then breaking these arguments apart only to reestablish them again to the amazement of all. None could defeat him in any branch of scholarship. Yet once he established himself, he discarded scholarship altogether. After his youthful years of study, he overtly took to the cause of devotion, and he did so with great intensity. Throughout his life he never wrote more than eight stanzas, each of which extolled the virtues of the culture of pure devotion and the act of invoking the name of God. Thus, he demonstrated that knowledge, which is so sought after by materialists and spiritual seekers alike, is not life's ultimate goal. Just as in the material plane, so in the spiritual world of Śrī Chaitanya, love does not answer to reason.

Together with his devotees, Śrī Chaitanya inaugurated the *dharma* of the age, *kṛṣṇa-saṅkīrtana,* congregational chanting of the names of God. Accepting the renounced order of life, *sannyāsa,* he toured the whole of India propagating the chanting of the Hare Kṛṣṇa *mahā-mantra.* While Europe was awakening to an era of speculation, Śrī Chaitanya ushered in a renaissance of devotion aimed at ending all speculation about the nature of truth.

The Hare Kṛṣṇa *mantra* is mentioned throughout the Vedic literature. In the *Kalī-Saṁtaraṇa Upaniṣad,* Nārada asks his father, Brahmā, about the means of deliverance in the Kali-yuga, the Vedic age of darkness which began five thousand years ago. Brahmā replied that chanting the name of God is most efficacious in this age. Nārada proceeded to inquire further as to which names in particular were most auspicious. Brahmā replied with the following verse:

hare kṛṣṇa hare kṛṣṇa
kṛṣṇa kṛṣṇa hare hare
hare rāma hare rāma
rāma rāma hare hare

iti ṣoḍaśakaṁ nāmnāṁ
kali-kalmaṣa nāśanam
nātah parataropayaḥ
sarva vedeṣu dṛśyate

"In all of the Vedas no better method for counteracting the effects of the Kali-yuga can be found than the chanting of these sixteen names of God: Hare Kṛṣṇa Hare Kṛṣṇa Kṛṣṇa Kṛṣṇa Hare Hare Hare Rāma Hare Rāma Rāma Rāma Hare Hare." Śrī Chaitanya chanted this *mantra* both congregationally in public *(kīrtana)* and privately on beads *(japa).*

Nowadays, few are totally unfamiliar with the Hare Kṛṣṇa *mantra.* It was made a household word in the 1960s and 1970s by the movement of A. C. Bhaktivedanta Swami Prabhupāda, which is popularly known as the Hare Kṛṣṇa movement. Despite its perceived shortcomings, this movement is a historical landmark. It fulfilled the 16th century prediction of Śrī Chaitanya recorded in the *Chaitanya Bhāgavata.* There, Śrī Chaitanya predicted that the Hare Kṛṣṇa *mantra* would be heard in every town and village on earth.

Transplanting a cultural movement onto foreign soil is no easy task. When the movement is more than cultural, when it is spiritual, the burden is by no means less. Bhaktivedanta Swami took up this task as a humble servant of Śrī Chaitanya in our times, some five hundred years after Śrī Chaitanya's divine advent. In a prayer composed in the Boston harbor, where he landed penniless in 1965, Bhaktivedanta Swami prayed for direction to accomplish this task, signing his poem "the most insignificant beggar." This spirit of humility characterizes the true followers of Śrī Chaitanya, who instructed his disciples in his famous eight prayers *(Śikśāṣṭakam)* to consider themselves "more humble than a blade of grass." Those who chant Hare Kṛṣṇa but do not think of themselves as such are at best only scratching the surface of this divine logos. It is understandable that a great spiritual idea is prone to being misunderstood. Certainly the Hare Kṛṣṇa movement has been misunderstood by the American public and to an extent by the movement's own adherents as well. Yet if we take Śrī Chaitanya seriously, we can be sure that Hare Kṛṣṇa is not going to go away. It is not a fad, but a factual statement about the emotional potential of our soul.

Invoking the name of God is common to a great number of religious traditions. Yet Śrī Chaitanya has expounded an entire theology centered on this common thread that runs through the diverse fabric of the world's spiritual traditions. His advocacy of chanting the name of Kṛṣṇa further attests to the unique contribution he made to the theistic world. Hare Kṛṣṇa represents the zenith of spiritual love, *gopībhāva,* or conjugal love of Godhead, the transcendental concept this book culminates in.

As a *sannyāsī,* Śrī Chaitanya strictly avoided associating with women for sex. He observed strict vows of celibacy throughout his renounced life. Yet his object of worship was Śrī Kṛṣṇa, the transcendental Cupid. He worshipped in the mood of a lover and advocated that the love of the *gopīs* (milkmaidens) of Vṛndāvana for Kṛṣṇa knew no equal.

From outside the Chaitanya tradition, Christian theologian John Moffitt expressed his view of Śrī Chaitanya in *Journey to Gorakhpur: An Encounter with Christ Beyond Christianity:*

> If I were asked to choose one man in Indian religious history who best represents the pure spirit of devotional self-giving, I would choose the Vaishnavite saint Caitanya, whose full name in religion was Krishna Caitanya, or

"Krishna consciousness." Of all the saints in recorded history, East or West, he seems to me the supreme example of a soul carried away on a tide of ecstatic love of God. This extraordinary man, who belongs to the rich period beginning with the end of the fourteenth century, represents the culmination of the devotional schools that grew up around Krishna.

When he debated with philosophers, Caitanya could be as scholarly as the great teachers, or *ācāryas*, of old—Sankara, Ramanuja, and Madhva. . . . In his teaching of the path of devotion to the general public, however, he continued to stress utter devotion to the Lord. This devotion was to be developed through hearing and singing the name and glories of Krishna, meditating on his form and attributes and his life on earth, worshipping him in his temples, resigning oneself to his will, trying to do only what would please him, serving his devotees, and showing kindness to all beings.

Caitanya aroused in his followers a flood of passionate love of God. As a result, a wave of religious fervor swept over Bengal and Orissa. Yet despite the emotionalism his teachings brought about, he himself was extremely strict. He closely watched the morals of those who were around him, sternly reproving any form of self-indulgence. Though literally worshipped by thousands as Krishna himself, he led a simple and even austere life.

Caitanya delighted intensely in nature. It is said that, like St. Francis of Assisi, he had a miraculous power over wild beasts. His life in the

> holy town of Puri is the story of a man in a state of almost continuous spiritual intoxication. Illuminating discourses, deep contemplation, moods of loving communion with God, were daily occurrences.

The insistence of those within the Gauḍīya Vaiṣṇava tradition that Śrī Chaitanya is Kṛṣṇa disguised as a devotee of himself is well supported. It has become fashionable to proclaim one's guru God incarnate (if the guru has not already done so). But claims by such so-called gurus and their foolish followers are usually not well-founded. In the case of Śrī Chaitanya, not only is there considerable scriptural support to substantiate this claim, but moreover the parallels between Kṛṣṇa's incarnation on earth and Śrī Chaitanya's some forty-five hundred years later are overwhelming.

For example, the *Bhāgavata* describes that when Kṛṣṇa appeared, so did all of his eternal associated *śaktis*, personified as his family and entourage. Kṛṣṇa's *ādhāra śakti,* or energy of support for the power of sustenance, is personified as his mother, Yaśodā, an eternal devotee in his transcendental pastimes. Similarly he has a father, friends, servants, and lovers, the principal of whom is Śrī Rādhā, the personified *hladhinī-śakti* (pleasure potency). All of these eternally associated energies of Kṛṣṇa appeared with him when he descended as Śrī Chaitanya. All of the lives of Śrī Chaitanya's intimate associates show strong parallels with corresponding associates of Kṛṣṇa mentioned in the *Bhāgavata.* The numerous self-proclaimed incarnations of "Kṛṣṇa" usually have, at best, a "Rādhā" in their lives, which makes things worse and such persons that much more questionable.[1]

1. Pseudo-incarnations of Kṛṣṇa often have a female associate with whom they engage in a sensuous relationship, imitating the transcendental pastimes of Rādhā-Kṛṣṇa. This is the height of hypocrisy.

In the personality of Kṛṣṇa we find a very different God from that of the Judeo-Christian tradition. He is also very different from anything we find in the pagan traditions, whose gods and goddesses clearly do not represent a wholly transcendental conception. There is greater similarity between Viṣṇu of Vaikuṇṭha and Kṛṣṇa, yet still a vast difference between the two. But Kṛṣṇa is not a different God from Viṣṇu, neither for that matter is he different from the Gods of other traditions. Thoughtful, objective analysis reveals that all Gods are but partial manifestations of the same *puruṣa,* Śrī Kṛṣṇa, and all Goddesses partial expressions of the primal *śakti,* Śrī Rādhā. Kṛṣṇa possesses all attributes of divinity found in other incarnations as well as aspects found in him alone. There can be only one God, yet as explained earlier, he has many expressions of himself.

In Rādhā-Kṛṣṇa we find complementary aspects of divinity, each interdependent on the other—potency and potent. Just as a teacher is meaningless without a student, and a student meaningless without a teacher, Rādhā and Kṛṣṇa give meaning to each another. They are one, but are expressed as two for the practical functioning of divinity in its pursuit of ecstasy.

In Kṛṣṇa we find a conception of Godhead that is far from uptight and sexually repressed. Kṛṣṇa appears to be very sexually active. But Śrī Chaitanya saves us from potential confusion about Kṛṣṇa. As Śrī Chaitanya was strictly celibate, shall we think that he worshipped sex? It is hardly possible to contemplate sexuality constantly within one's mind and yet be sexually inactive in the realm of the body and senses. Therefore, in his advocacy of Rādhā-Kṛṣṇa, Śrī Chaitanya points to the spiritual origins of our sexuality in transcendence. He says that the soul has emotions, that sexuality is a component of the soul, not of the flesh as other spiritual traditions would have us believe. Moreover, he says that this emotive component is ultimately what the soul is all about. It is no wonder then that we are preoccupied with sexuality. It is, as many sense, the essence of our spirituality. Yet, lacking knowledge, most progressive spiritual seekers remain unfulfilled, relegating all emotive experience to the realm of illusion and thinking that spirituality is ultimately a void.

Voidism and its sister monism have been dismissed thus far as nonmaterial yet not wholly spiritual notions. Western spiritual tradition is vague in its description of a personal God. This is so much so that those who truly pursue experiential Christianity, for example, often end up concurring with nondualists as to the nature of the spiritual experience. Rāmānuja's Viṣṇu, the God of the Vaiṣṇavas, with his consort Lakṣmī is a novel idea in the West, but an idea that is well-represented with logic and scriptural basis. Yet the concept of Rādhā-Kṛṣṇa presented by Śrī Chaitanya takes us the final step in finding a God of love. His followers, even while possessed of that love, are not without an explanation of Śrī Chaitanya's conception of divine love, which tests the measure of our logic and scriptural command.

The *Bhāgavata* states, *kṛṣṇas tu bhagavān svayam*. "Kṛṣṇa is the original Godhead." *Original* means that he is the origin of all other forms of Godhead. All forms of Godhead originate in him. Anything that we find in Rāma, Viṣṇu, Śiva, or any of the expressions of Godhead are also found in Kṛṣṇa, yet in Kṛṣṇa we find something more. In Rūpa Goswāmī's *Bhakti-rasāmṛta-sindhu*, we find a description of some of the transcendental qualities of Śrī Kṛṣṇa. A comparison is made between Kṛṣṇa and the living entities. In their purified consciousness, the living entities can possess in a minute degree fifty of the sixty-four principal transcendental qualities that Kṛṣṇa possesses in full.

The original Godhead, Kṛṣṇa, the source of all *avatāras*, or incarnations, possesses unlimited qualities. Theological infinity is very different from mathematical infinity. Mathematical infinity implies having no limits whatsoever. In a theological infinity; however, Godhead is "definite"—he has character, and in this sense he is limited. Yet he is unlimited in that he is immeasurable, and nothing exists outside of him that can limit him. In him all things are contained—unlimited beauty, unlimited strength, unlimited knowledge, unlimited charm, and so on. All good and all so-called bad is harmonized in him.

Transcendental qualities are in one sense not different from mundane qualities. They differ only in that they are properly adjusted in relation to the center of all things. In the plane of material experience, all qualities are only shadows of the actual qualities they reflect. It is farcical if, after robbing a bank, thieves insist among themselves on dividing the spoils "honestly." Similarly, all things belong to God. If we see them otherwise, that is criminal. All of our so-called good qualities are tarnished by the spiritually criminal basis of our material existence, an existence based on a false sense of proprietorship.

In the presence of the proprietor of all things, who shows himself as time and death in this world, the good or bad qualities we possess are revealed for what they are: our imagination about ourselves. The truth—that we are servants of Godhead—is made obvious by time and tide, which wait for no man or woman. When we recognize that everything belongs to God and live a life in concert with this truth, we can develop transcendental qualities—qualities that arise out of being conscious of the absolute proprietorship of Godhead.

It is important to consider that "good" or "bad" qualities are relative to that which they are centered on. Honesty, although a good quality, is not good at all if it arises out of criminality. Similarly, bad qualities such as dishonesty that leads to theft is not bad if properly centered. To steal from oneself is but harmless play. Thus transcendence must ultimately be the reversal of the tide of material existence. Transcendence necessarily includes all qualities, both so-called good and bad, harmonized for ultimate good. Conversely, material existence, with all of its goods and bads, is all bad, for it is all off-center.

This is relevant to the Kṛṣṇa conception of Godhead, for Kṛṣṇa has been described not only in terms of good qualities, but also as a thief, debauchee, and many other ordinarily undesirable qualities. Kṛṣṇa is the boy who stole the young milkmaidens' clothing while they bathed. He danced with many young ladies in the village of Vṛndāvana, only to leave them and marry so many princesses in Dvārakā. As Godhead has qualities, so he also has activities *(līlās)*, all of which are transcendental. They are transcendental because they are beyond the limits of time and space he imposes upon those who are not conscious of his ultimate proprietorship. Time and space amount to our sentence and cell in our term of incarceration within material existence. But just as there is life within prison, there is life outside the prison walls. Kṛṣṇa *līlā* is not material *(prākṛta)*; it is supramundane *(aprākṛta)*. It resembles the mundane plane, yet it is altogether different.

In the Kṛṣṇa conception of Godhead, all things are harmonized. Love of Kṛṣṇa is not devoid of any of the qualities we find in ordinary mundane love. This is quite different from the personal God of Christianity or the Viṣṇu of Vaikuṇṭha. Ordinarily, when we think of loving God we think of a kind of love that excludes certain undeniable elements of mundane love. For example, in our material experience, lovers quarrel. But we do not ordinarily think of quarreling with God. The general conception of love of God is a sterile one, from which many elements of mundane love have been extracted. Transcendental love of Kṛṣṇa, however, leaves nothing out. It is different from mundane love only at its foundation, leaving the entire structure of love in place.

The foundation of mundane love is self-centeredness. It is centered on an erroneous conception of self arrived at through association with matter. As explained earlier, the senses afford us a distorted picture of reality. Under their influence we establish relationships with other embodied souls in order to satisfy the demands of the senses and the mind. These demands include emotional needs as well as physical needs. Driven by the senses we come close to others physically, yet often alienate ourselves from one another in reality on the spiritual plane. The soul expressing herself through the veil of the material senses finds little solace. If she divorces herself from her emotional potential altogether, she is left unfulfilled spiritually, for a voidistic or monistic conception of spirituality does not address the deepest voice of the soul.[2] The soul exists *(sat)*, and the soul can realize the truth of her existence *(cit)*, thus transcending death. But the purpose for which the soul exists is not merely peace, but emotional fulfillment, or joy *(ānandam)*.

Undoubtedly, there is joy in knowing that we do not have to die (self-realization), but it is a watered-down joy that is abstract at best. *Brahman*, the undifferentiated pure consciousness that underlies the material manifestation, is an abstract expression of joy. It is impersonal. The undiluted form of consciousness is the personality of Godhead, Bhagavān, bliss personified. The impersonal expression of ourselves is only a partial expression of our being. It is

2. Here emotional potential refers to the potential of the soul to experience emotional fulfillment beyond embodied material life in a transcendental relationship *(rasa)* with Kṛṣṇa.

contained within our personhood. Similarly, in the impersonal *Brahman,* the personhood of Godhead is not present in full. As Viṣṇu or Narāyaṇa, his personality is more fully expressed. But as Śrī Kṛṣṇa, the personality of Godhead is expressed in full.

All that we know to be elements of "love" from our experience in this world have their expression in the absolute spiritual love of Kṛṣṇa and his devotees. This includes so-called negative aspects of love, such as jealousy, envy, anger, lust, and other such undeniable elements of loving reciprocation. Every nuance of emotional experience is realized in perfection within the Kṛṣṇa conception of Godhead. Rasa, transcendental relationship, finds it fullest expression in the Kṛṣṇa conception.

This truth was expressed by Śrī Chaitanya like the flowing of a waterfall. His principal disciples, the six Goswāmīs of Vṛndāvana, channeled that waterfall into the lake of the Gauḍīya Vaiṣṇava *sampradāya* such that others could drink Śrī Chaitanya's doctrine of divine love. The contribution of Jīva Goswāmī has already been mentioned. He was the nephew and follower of Rūpa and Sanātana Goswāmīs. Ragunātha dāsa, Gopāla Bhaṭṭa, and Ragunātha Bhaṭṭa were their companions, and together they effectively established the lineage. All of these saints appeared in this world, as did Śrī Chaitanya, as mendicants *(sannyāsīs)* who appeared to renounce the world but, in fact, embraced the world in accord with the teaching of Śrī Chaitanya. It is only their vision of the world that differs from ours—a difference that at its heart acknowledges our sexual-emotive drive as having spiritual origins in the *hlādinī-śakti,* the pleasure potency of Śrī Kṛṣṇa.

There is much mystery to the appearance of Śrī Chaitanya. He is a difficult person to understand. He renounced worldly dealings and sexual indulgence, yet he was simultaneously absorbed in contemplating the apparently sexual love of Rādhā-Kṛṣṇa. He is Godhead himself, yet at the same time he was the ideal worshipper of God. At times he denied his Godhood, while at other times he acknowledged it. By material analysis he appears to be schizophrenic, a split personality, mad yet profound at the same time. But mundane one-dimensional assessments of anything fall short, especially one-dimensional assessments of spiritual phenomena.

We have examined the idea of God as a person, concluding that the personhood of Godhead is his lovable aspect. From his personhood, all transcendentally lesser manifestations of God emanate. There are lesser and greater manifestations of God and gradations of standing in transcendence. Transcendence is not a blur of undifferentiated oneness. It is filled with unlimited variegatedness, the foundation for which is *advaya-jñāna* (nondual knowledge). Nondual here refers to the illusory duality that arises from material sense perception. The fountainhead of transcendence is the person of Śrī Kṛṣṇa. He is the source of God, Viṣṇu, and as such his Godhood and divinity are somewhat difficult to detect. "God," in a sense, is a partial expression of Kṛṣṇa, who is intrinsically joy personified experiencing himself eternally in ever new pastimes. Yet Kṛṣṇa is God, in that it is joy by which all things are ultimately controlled. Joy rules our life. We move for its sake, and nothing is allowed to interfere with its pursuit. Even if we look for pain, it is joy we are seeking in a perverted way.

Yet if God is conceived of as the personification of joy, he must also be regarded as the highest love, which produces the greatest joy. Śrī Rādhā is the highest love in person. Rādhā-Kṛṣṇa, ecstasy and love, *mahābhāva* and *rasarāja,* are two necessary complementary constituents of the absolute. When the joy Śrī Rādhā derives from loving Kṛṣṇa becomes apparent to him, he naturally desires to experience that himself. Thus, as described by Kṛṣṇadāsa Kavirāja Goswāmī, the author of *Śrī Caitanya-caritāmṛta* (the most widely recognized biography of Śrī Chaitanya), when Kṛṣṇa desires to taste himself and experience the joy that Śrī Rādhā knows in loving him, he accepts her disposition. This union of the mind of Śrī Rādhā and the form of Kṛṣṇa is Śrī Chaitanya. The overflow of this transcendental love showers down upon the material world in the form of his divine dispensation, kṛṣṇa-saṅkīrtana. The dark Lord, Śrī Kṛṣṇa, becomes golden, bearing the complexion of Śrī Rādhā. He is the Lord loving himself, teaching us the highest devotion, which brings the greatest joy.

The conclusions of the *Caitanya-caritāmṛta* are based on the *Bhāgavata.* References such as *kṛṣṇa-varṇaṁ tviṣākṛṣṇaṁ* (SB 11.5.32), *āsan varṇās trayo hy asya* (SB 10.8.13), and *channaḥ kalau* (SB 7.9.38) all make clear reference to the disguised appearance of Kṛṣṇa in Kali-yuga. But more important to our discussion is the *Bhāgavata's* reference to Śrī Rādhā, *ārādhanam,* as the one by whom Kṛṣṇa is best worshipped, the one who completely conquers him by her love. This is the teaching of Śrī Chaitanya through which the answer to the mystery of life is solved. That we live for love cannot be denied. How to realize the perfection of love can be understood through the example of Śrī Chaitanya, following in the footsteps of Śrī Rādhā.

8

RASA: LOVE RELATIONSHIPS IN TRANSCENDENCE

The Bhāgavata *emphasizes the theory of rasa referred to in the* Taittirīya Upaniṣad, raso vai saḥ. *Rasa means juice or taste. It represents the essential in anything we experience, the feeling of anything. In the Bhāgavata philosophy, it refers to the ultimate aesthetic experience in transcendence—loving relationship with Godhead, the emotional fulfillment of the soul.*

Material relationships leave us unfulfilled. They have little to do with ourselves, our souls. The soul is like a valuable diamond. In the material plane of experience, that diamond is covered by a mountain of misconception. The senses, the mental system, and the intellect all cover the soul, who expresses herself through them in search of *rasa. Rasa* means the mellow that we derive from being in touch with any particular thing. It is not the object itself we seek to possess, but the aesthetic experience derived from contacting any particular object. That experience is *rasa,* the mellow or taste arising out of any relationship.

Our relationship with matter cannot produce *rasa* that is fulfilling. We are living, and matter is dead. Similarly, as much as we identify with matter (the body, mind, and intellect), we are close to death. Two people close to death cannot give much life to one another. *Raso vai saḥ,* the *Upaniṣads* declare. We live for *rasa. Rasa* is what life is about. But we cannot experience the fulfillment of *rasa* while dwelling in material consciousness. In the material plane, in relationship to dull matter and other souls dulled by matter, we can find only the *rasa,* or aesthetic experience, of disgust.

This is so because the whole affair is a sham. We have been invited to dinner, but the host is feeding us only appetizers, with the promise of a meal to come. We may even smell the cooking, but in time we will realize only indigestion. There is no square meal for the soul in the material plane of consciousness. There is no *rasa ānandam,* no aesthetic experience of joy that endures. Neither do the fleeting pleasures of the material experience completely fulfill one while they last. Often while experiencing material pleasure, we are thinking about something yet to come.

Undeniably, there is some pleasure in the material experience. This is so because the material nature is the *śakti* of Godhead, who in his most original expression is Śrī Kṛṣṇa, *rasarāja,* the reservoir of *rasa. Akhila-rasāmṛta mūrti* (BRS 1.1), Kṛṣṇa is the very form of aesthetic joy. The material experience is not divorced from him altogether. It is one dimension of the totality of experience. And Kṛṣṇa is the reservoir of all experience.

If we are to find fulfillment, we must look beyond the material range of experience. We must look beyond the fact that material experience in itself is unfulfilling (a disappointing truth that leads to frustration), and not stop short in our pursuit of *rasa* by becoming ensnared in intellectual meandering leading to voidism. But how can we look beyond our experience? This is the beauty of the *Bhāgavata,* for it tells that the truth is self-evident.

When we speak of the absolute truth, we speak of that which is already existing. Holy books do not contain the truth, although truth is to one degree or another discussed in them. As the *Bhāgavata* points out, truth exists independently of scripture, *śrutibhir vimṛgyām* (SB 10.47.61). Saints and scriptures only point out that which is already before our eyes, redirecting our angle of vision. Saints often do this with the help of metaphors that draw upon our human experience. Just as we can learn something about water by studying ice, we can learn about the truth by studying illusion, because material existence is the ice of the pure water of our spirituality. Human experience is the imprint of the divine, as God made man and woman in his and her image. Therefore, we can conceive of the nature of absolute truth in a hazy way from within the framework of the relative truth of our human experience.

No doubt, a hazy conception of the truth is insufficient to inspire the necessary action that delivers the goal of life. Proper conceptualization requires the help of saints and scriptures, and acquiring their grace enables us to actualize the truth of our soul. Yet, being suspicious as we are, living in a land of doubt, often causes us to question and even challenge our own well-wishers. Left with our human experience and our firm faith in the same, we should be at least willing to examine that experience objectively and then exchange notes with the *ṛṣis.*

We know that we exist. Cognition *(cit)* and existence *(sat)* are essential aspects of our being. However, mere cognizance that we exist is incomplete—we exist for a purpose. That purpose is emotional fulfillment *(ānanda).* Whatever wonderful feat one accomplishes, be it a record-breaking exhibition of physical prowess in the field of athletics or an intellectual breakthrough in the laboratory, it is the emotional fulfillment that we receive from these activities that gives them meaning. When a baseball player hits a home run with two outs in the bottom of the ninth to win the game, the distance, speed, and trajectory of the ball are all meaningless facts when viewed separately from the emotional fulfillment surrounding the event. When the crowd roars, the confetti flies, and tears flow, the event has meaning. Similarly, when a scientist discovers a fact after years of research, only when he or she can share it with others, and feel in their association the excitement of the finding, is the emotional fulfillment complete.

We live for love. We live in search of emotional fulfillment. No man is an island, no woman alone. If we do seem at times to seek aloneness, it is only because our attempts for relationships have been fraught with the shortcomings of a life that does not endure, a life that is off-center. The frustration that ensues from material relationships does not in itself hold the potential to reveal the nature of the whole truth, and half truth may be worse than no truth at all. If, after many lifetimes of seeking love through material relationships, one realizes that all material relationships fall short and do not endure, one may drift toward the half-truth of impersonalism and voidism in the name of spirituality. The whole truth is that we will only thrive when we find the relationship in which there is no shortcoming, when we learn to love Godhead.

From a religious point of view, lawless love is the height of immorality. Married love is proper, but attachment to one's partner is the heart of the knot of material bondage. Attachment to children is purer, for when attachment for wife or husband is transferred to the children, sexual exploitation of one's partner is often left behind. Parental love also requires greater sacrifice, greater giving with less expectation of reward. Relationships with friends are higher yet because in this type of relationship we often discuss matters of truth and aid one another in truth's pursuit with a greater sense of detachment from one another. In friendly dealings, we sense more readily the impermanence of the relationship and think of it more philosophically. The relationship between teacher and student is even higher, for ultimately in this relationship we find out definitively about the truth. In the optimum, when the teacher is a self-realized soul, the student is led to spiritual peace. Thus the relationship that brings peace holds the highest position in the plane of material experience. But if material life is the reflection of the spiritual, in the spiritual realm peace will find its place at the bottom of the structure of love, while lawless love rises to the top. The evidence of this truth is found by thoroughly examining the shadow of truth, which is expressed in the material plane.

In the material plane, again and again, we try to love—as children, parents, friends, and lovers. Spirituality aside, if we look closely at our human experience, we have to conclude that to the extent that any of these kinds of relationships are fulfilling, our lives are meaningful. All else may be lost, but if we have loved successfully, we consider our lives complete.

In all of our attempts for love, the love between man and woman, conjugal love, holds the greatest potential for emotional fulfillment. We love our parents, yet in childhood we are unable to address every aspect of our guardian's emotional needs. As we grow and make friends, we love them. Our parents in later life also become our friends. Yet among friends we find a best friend, who becomes our lover, and with whom we share most intimately. Thus, sexual love is the climax of loving exchange. In that relationship, we may also bear children and love them, and although this love is potentially more fulfilling, more consuming, than that of friend and friend, it recedes to the background when our emotional needs call out to be fulfilled as they can only be in the embrace of our lover.

The relationship between lovers heightens with the addition of certain elements of risk. Married life, while emotionally fulfilling, lends to familiarity and its initial intention is eventually compromised as the needs of raising a family make their demands. When family encumbrances are absent and couples risk condemnation, lawless love, decadent as it is, offers even greater potential for emotional fulfillment. For this kind of love, we risk everything, because through it we gain more fully that which we are seeking in everything else we do. If the president of the United States, who has sometimes been described as the most powerful man on earth, should fall in love with a woman other than his wife, he stands to lose everything if anyone finds out about his affair. But will he give her up for his presidency? If he really falls in love with her, he won't, because he has found the fulfillment of his heart, a love that knows no reason.

Our human experience dictates that truth is the love between man and woman. No subject has been written about more often, no thought contemplated more frequently. Out of this affair, entire countries have risen and fallen. All the lower species—the plants, the birds, the bees, and the beasts—are the backdrop of this reality. When a young man picks a rose from a garden and places it in his young lover's hair, that flower reaches new aesthetic heights it could not have realized otherwise. The entire creation is moving in concert: birds chirping, bees humming, energizing the love of man for woman, woman for man.

Of course, if we stop at an anthropocentric worldview, our analysis of the human experience falls short. As mentioned earlier, our pursuit of human emotional fulfillment is not without its problems, for in the very least our participation in it may be interrupted at any moment. We may not believe in God, but we cannot ignore death and, at the same time, accurately deduce the nature of truth from examining our human experience. But we would be wrong to conclude that reasoning and knowledge should rule our lives, rather than love and service. Reasoning dictates that human love is temporary, but only poor reasoning tells us that love and all of its emotional nuances are illusion, that to pursue love is to pursue illusion. With the exercise of powerful reasoning, the utter futility of a life ruled by the heart, in a world in which all relationships are temporal, becomes apparent. Yet are we to conclude that our entire human experience with all of its varied emotional flutters is all false? Is there no truth in what we feel? Love is the king to whom reason is an advisor, an advisor who may or may not be necessary. Misdirected love can take help from reasoning, while love properly centered needs little help from our discriminating faculty. The truth lies in directing our love to the proper center, not in foregoing love out of frustration.

What we see and feel is not false; we have merely drawn our perception from the wrong angle. The truth is before our eyes. It is not that by philosophizing away everything in our human experience we will arrive at the truth. Rather by fully embracing our human experience, which is the ice of the water of our spirituality, we will come to know the truth about ourselves. Ice is nothing but water, yet we cannot use ice as water until we melt it. Similarly, the entire range of human emotions and our constant pursuit of love are all elements of the truth, but our hearts are frozen in the idea that we are the center. But are we individually or collectively the center of all things? Life on earth may revolve around the human love affair, but death on earth should lead us to conclude that human life is not the center of reality. Time and death tell us that there is a superior controlling agency that has jurisdiction over our life and love.

Our human experience leads us to conclude that we must make absolute that which we find to be the most emotionally fulfilling. We must center the emotionally fulfilling experience of lawless love on that which has jurisdiction over our human affairs. We are not the owners and controllers of all things. It is only envy that leads us to conclude that nothing else is in control. It is frustration in our personal relationships that brings us to the erroneous conclusion that this superior agency possesses anything less than we do, that it is devoid of personality. This superior controlling agency, or, ultimately, person, is he to whom all things belong. It is no wonder that he seems unfriendly to us—cruel death—tearing us from our loved ones. We have taken the position that all things belong to us. Perhaps we should learn to love that controlling agency, beginning by recognizing that nothing really belongs to us.

The transcendentalists tell us that we have created the experience of death by embracing the wrong angle of vision. It is a vision born out of faulty sense perception. Through the senses, we, the conscious being, contact the external world—touching, tasting, smelling, seeing, and so on. This contact relays messages to the mind, which in turn accepts or rejects an experience as good or bad, happy or sad. In this way, we create a world of likes and dislikes. It is a world of dualities in which I am the Lord. It is my world, my reality—yet hardly the truth. With my meager purpose of fulfilling my sensual demands, I march off exploiting all, animate and inanimate, as the Lord of all I survey. As I do, so do others, and thus there are more than one too many Lords of this way of life. We may not believe in God, yet only inasmuch as we try to be God ourselves. One God we can have, one center. The center must be one, while the circumference has no limit. Harmony requires one Lord, yet the more subordinates the better.

When we fully awaken the cognitive factor of the soul, the threat of nonexistence dissolves. When I know that I cannot die, all fear disappears and the struggle for existence ends. The war is over, but life without war is another experience altogether. As we know, life means love, but real life is love absolute. In the world of the five senses and the mind, we have only a shadowy experience of existence, a dim sense of security. Our knowledge is ignorance, and our love for one is often hate for another.

If we are to pursue emotional fulfillment, as we must, we should do it in such a way that it brings us in connection with that which is eternal. When we begin to love the Absolute Godhead, an overwhelming sense of gratitude will fill our hearts. A great burden, the root cause of all our fear and anxiety, will be unearthed, as the threat of death turns into the relief of eternal life, peace at last. From gratitude to service, love thickens. Ultimately, we can make Godhead our lover, ourselves the beloved. Yet this natural conclusion, derived from an objective look at our human experience, without the help of religious books or saints, stands in opposition to most standard interpretations of scripture and the words of the saints.

As mentioned earlier, great realizers speak not only from their particular level of ascent on the mountain of truth, but in consideration of time and circumstances as well. They may know more than what they tell us. The dissemination of truth is the untiring work of Godhead himself, who does so through a multitude of agents, as he sees fit. But has any one of them spoken of lawless love of God as the zenith of theism? Most advocate peace, spiritual equanimity, and a relationship with God as master, ourselves as servant.

Ādi Śaṅkara and his monistic *advaitavāda* follower's conception of reality leaves no room for emotion, attributes, form, or even Godhead himself, what to speak of God's servants. Rāmānuja, Madhva, and other Vaiṣṇava *ācāryas* pay little or no attention to this revolutionary concept of absolutizing our emotional drive such that it culminates in lawless love. Rāmānuja considers devotion in awe and reverence the highest. Madhva does not speak about lawless love. General theism cringes at such thoughts. Love of God is agape, without similarity to human sexual love. Although less than a handful of Catholic saints do hint vaguely at the idea of becoming the bride of Christ, lawless love, paramour love, is unthinkable.

Not so for Śrī Chaitanya, the emblem of love divine around whom the Gauḍīya Vaiṣṇavas unite. If God is mentioned with reference to a spiritual sexuality, as in Christianity or any other tradition, Śrī Chaitanya's doctrine is the flower of the seed of such conceptions. He and his band of followers made the truth of conjugal love the central theme of their mission. In doing so they presented a tightly reasoned and scripturally backed philosophy of divine love. Yet while pointing to the obvious truth of our human experience, they were ever so careful to differentiate divine love from human love of the senses. It may be similar, but not the same. *Kāma* is not *prema*: lust is not love, one is the reflection of the other. This is not the difference between agape and sexual love, inasmuch as at a glance prema in its highest expression closely resembles mundane love. Love of Viṣṇu may be analogous to agape, but not *kṛṣṇa prema* of *mādhurya rasa,* or conjugal love.

This love is most fully expressed in the figure of Śrī Rādhā. Her *prema* of *mahābhāva* fully captivates Śrī Kṛṣṇa. She is the pleasure potency, *hlādinī-śakti,* of the Lord, and from her the potential for the *jīva* souls to experience pleasure expands. She is the spiritual source of our sexual drive, which moves off-center when we are in contact with material nature, *māyā-śakti.* Properly centered this innate drive for pleasure takes one to the eternal *līlās* of Rādhā-Kṛṣṇa.

Just as the mundane world is pervaded by sexual desire, the transcendental realm of Rādhā-Kṛṣṇa is ruled by *mādhurya,* which is none other than the full face of our innate drive for pleasure *(ādi-rasa).* In the highest spiritual realm, all five of the basic *rasas* are eternally manifest. *Śānta-rasa, dāsya-rasa, sākhya-rasa,* and *vātsalya-rasa* all form the stage, background, and secondary characters necessary for the drama of *mādhurya* to unfold. The spiritual realm of Rādhā-Kṛṣṇa exists in a dimension beyond the dualities of material existence *(śānta).* Service is the underlying spirit *(dāsya).* Friendship indirectly assists *(sākhya),* while paternal love often interferes for further accent *(vātsalya).* All of these transcendental relationships with the Lord are complete in themselves. They exist eternally in the heart of Śrī Kṛṣṇa and are realized by his devotees in the course of their spiritual evolution. Yet all *rasas* assist *mādhurya,* which is central to the divine realm. The apparently inanimate objects, trees, waters, and stones are not so. They are devotees in *śānta rasa.* The servants of Kṛṣṇa are situated in *dāsya rasa,* his friends in *sākhya rasa,* and his elders in *vātsalya rasa.* But the essential elements that these *rasas* consist of are all present in *mādhurya rasa,* which also contains elements not found in the other four primary *rasas.* Thus *mādhurya rasa* is the apex of spiritual attainment, which pervades the divine abode of Śrī Kṛṣṇa, just as mundane sexual love is what material existence is all about.

To describe Śrī Chaitanya's conception of divine love in terms we might understand, Rūpa Goswāmī borrowed from the secular version of *rasa* found in orthodox poetry. Making necessary modifications, he constructed a framework to explain the theory of transcendental *rasa* mentioned in the *Bhāgavata.* In so doing, he and his followers have been careful to distinguish Kṛṣṇa's spiritual love relationship with the milkmaids of Vraja from the affairs of ordinary men and women. Kṛṣṇa's transcendental love affairs have been misunderstood by scholars and have been abused as a license for sensual indulgence in the name of spiritual pursuit. Although they bear the same outward resemblance, Kṛṣṇa's love affairs are categorically different from the "love" between illusioned souls. The love between illusioned souls, which mundane poets praise, is activated by the demands of our material senses. The result of these sensual demands is off-center relationships. This includes platonic relationships based on intellectual stimuli. Such relationships do not endure and cannot fulfill the soul. But a relationship with the transcendental Deity is properly centered. God is the center, and to perceive otherwise is illusion. Only when we understand this point and relate with one another accordingly can our relationships be considered spiritual. Caitanya-caritāmṛta cautions us thus:

sahaja gopīra prema,
nahe prākṛta kāma
kāma-kriḍā-sāmye tāra
kahi 'kāma'-nāma

"The natural love of the *gopīs* for Kṛṣṇa is not mundane lust. It is called *kāma* (lust) because it appears to resemble lusty affairs." (Cc. M. 8.215) Śukadeva Goswāmī confirms this in his concluding words to the essential chapters of the *Śrīmad Bhāgavatam* dealing with Kṛṣṇa's conjugal love affairs. There he says:

vikrīditaṁ vraja-vadhūbhir idaṁ ca viṣṇoḥ
śraddhānvito 'nuśṛṇuyād atha varṇayed yaḥ
bhaktiṁ parāṁ bhagavati pratilabhya kāmaṁ
hṛd-rogam āśv apahinoty acireṇa dhīraḥ

"Anyone who hears or describes the Lord's playful affairs with the young *gopīs* of Vṛndāvana will attain the Lord's pure devotional service. Thus he or she will quickly become sober and conquer lust, the disease of the heart." (SB 10.33.39) Here *śraddhā* means faith that Kṛṣṇa is the transcendental personality of Godhead, and *anu* means to follow the disciplic succession, *guru paramparā.* Faith in Kṛṣṇa awakens in connection with the genuine spiritual guide in the lineage of Śrī Chaitanya. If we continue to follow his or her guidance, hearing about the pastimes of Kṛṣṇa, our material lust will be converted into love of God.

Śrī Chaitanya was an ideal renunciate, as were his principal disciples, the legendary six Goswāmīs of Vṛndāvana. Externally, they were uninvolved in social and family affairs, what to speak of extramarital indulgence. Internally, they participated in the divine *līlās* of Kṛṣṇa and his milkmaids, the *gopīs.* Thus they worshipped *parakīyā-bhāva* in its pristine expression in transcendence. *Parakīyā-bhāva* is the pinnacle of theistic evolution *(ramya kācid upāsana vraja-vadhū-vargeṇā va kalpitā).*

Parakīyā means belonging to someone else. In Kṛṣṇa's Vṛndāvana pastimes, *parakīyā* touches all of his devotees in their different relationships with him, but it reaches its peak in *mādhurya,* or conjugal love. Kṛṣṇa's conjugal lovers, the *gopīs,* were not married to him. They appeared to belong to others and were in some cases already married. In principle all things are *svakīyā,* or "belonging" to Kṛṣṇa, yet in the divine play, the gopīs in particular appear to be spoken for. This sense of their belonging to another serves to intensify their love for Kṛṣṇa. This is not moral corruption; however, because all things, the gopīs and their so-called husbands as well, belong to Kṛṣṇa. It is only to experience greater intensity of *rasa* that Kṛṣṇa pretends that everything does not belong to him. The beauty of this transcendental truth of the pastimes of Kṛṣṇa is that hearing about it saves one from both moral corruption and the constraints of a life of moral adherence.

In revealing the esoteric truth of *parakīyā-bhāva,* Śrī Chaitanya has pointed to what is already before our eyes. He has only sought to adjust the angle of our vision. Others, such as Śaṅkara and his host of monistic followers, have labored to tell us that our human experience is all false, and that knowledge is our goal, not emotional fulfillment. They have troubled themselves much for very little. Theirs is a forced reading of reality. But Śrī Chaitanya has pointed out, as audacious as it may seem, that which is readily our experience: that truth is all about amorous love. He offers an entirely positive understanding of our sexuality—that it springs from Śrī Kṛṣṇa's pleasure potency, *hlādinī-śakti.* Sexuality is not something to be abandoned and condemned, but rather uncovered from the blanket of material nature. If we understand mundane sexuality for what it is, overwhelming inspiration to follow it to its natural spiritual conclusion will arise. Without this, moralistic repression or self-denying asceticism that leads to voidism will impede our natural spiritual evolution. To begin this spiritual evolution, we need only hear about the transcendental pastimes of Rādhā-Kṛṣṇa through the lineage of Śrī Chaitanya and embrace the path of *rāgānugā-bhakti.*

9

FROM POSTMODERNISM TO PREMA-DHARMA

As we move rapidly toward the twenty-first century, historians tell us that postmodern times are upon us. Just what these times hold for us, however, is debatable. The shortcomings of science, the dominant religion of the modern era, lie not in a short list of accomplishments. Modern science has brought us many tangibles. It is for this reason and the initial feeling that modern science's objectivity offered the potential to unite all humanity around facts, freeing us from superstition and subjectivity, that science was able to win so many converts from premodern times.

The common ground of knowing offered by modern science, however, centers around knowing that which offers little to improve the quality of our lives. Science is concerned with quantity, not quality. The intrinsic values of life are vastly important to us, yet about them modern science tells us nothing. The fault then of modern science is not its own, rather it lies in our overestimation of its worth. Modern science can reveal little if anything about the meaning of life. Thus many foresee a new era characterized by people returning to essential values. This is the result of realizing that after over two hundred reason-ruled scientific-industrial years, humanity is morally and spiritually bankrupt. Postmodernism may be only the dawning of this new era characterized by essential values and a common understanding of our spirituality.

Values are of course different for different people. For some, religion is foremost. Others value economic well-being. Others value facility for sense indulgence. Others value the noble yet abstract idea of freedom. Indian philosophy labels these four goals of human life *dharma, artha, kāma,* and *mokṣa*—religiosity, economic development, sense gratification, and liberation. These four values are often pursued over lifetimes, beginning with *dharma* and ending in *mokṣa.*

It could be said that the United States has since the time of its inception until the present gone through the cycle from *dharma* to *mokṣa.* As we enter postmodernism, the U.S. is now experiencing the desire for liberation having passed through religiosity, economic development, and sense indulgence. The founding fathers' conception gave rise to such slogans as, "In God we trust," and "One nation under God." But God was prayed to for material betterment. The long-range effect of this has been considerable economic development *(artha).* Those born after World War II took birth in a nation that was about to or already oozing with opportunities for sense indulgence *(kāma).* As we turn to postmodern times, frustration with sense indulgence, which inevitably alienates us from one another, is gradually creeping up on us. Thus many are seeking liberation *(mokṣa),* not through sense indulgence (free love), but from the shallowness of a skin-deep approach to life.

The desire for liberation is a desire to leave a shallow life behind, yet it is also shallow in terms of its spiritual content. The desire for liberation from a frustrating life of senseless sensuality cannot afford one fulfillment of the soul. The desire for liberation contains nothing positive, rather it is a form of negative theology that turns to rejecting the God we once prayed to for the wrong thing. Starting out on the wrong foot, we go down the wrong path. When we reach a dead end, we may foolishly reject the starting point, rather than the wrong step we took. God should be approached, but not for assisting us in our material pursuit. If we approach God for assistance in material pursuit, we will surely in time get the economic facility we so desire. Yet after enjoying our senses for some time, frustration sets in and the idea of God as a person is rejected. God is then replaced with a sophisticated philosophy in which we conveniently become God (the *Brahman)*, having done away with the so-called childish idea of his personhood.

In order to save us from doing away with the only hope for a life of love (the personality of Godhead), Śrī Chaitanya has introduced his conception of *prema-dharma. Prema-dharma* is very different from the ordinary *dharma* of religious adherence. The *Bhāgavata* labels popular religion *"kaitava-dharma"* or "cheating religion." It is a spirituality in which one is not willing to leave the physical plane. In this approach to God, we seek to engage God in helping us to fulfill a material objective. In its crudest form, one petitions the Lord for money—*dharma* for *artha.*

Materialistic religion often turns to imitation of genuine spirituality. Being unwilling to undergo the fire of ordeal (sacrificing our sense desire for the desires of Godhead) inevitably turns to distorting basic spiritual truth. "You can't take it with you" turns to a best-of-both-worlds scenario. This scenario sounds good to those addicted to material indulgence, but it sorely lacks philosophical support. Thus the differentiation between matter and consciousness is blurred, and spirituality is adulterated by the uncontrolled mind, wedded as it is to the senses.

Kaitava-dharma is not necessarily a particular brand of religion that does not lead to transcendence, such as Christian fundamentalism or many of the popular psycho-spiritual paths found in the human potential movement now known as the "new age." *Kaitava-dharma* can, and often is, expressed within a spiritual-conceptual framework that advocates genuine transcendence. Śrī Chaitanya's conception is no exception. Many people within what may be the broadest spiritual-conceptual framework may be in reality practicing *kaitava-dharma.* Śrī Chaitanya's doctrine of divine love is particularly liable to misunderstanding by those embodied in material consciousness. Many pseudosects appeared after his disappearance from the world that tried to make his divine theology a religion of the flesh or a means to an economic end. Thus kaitava-dharma is essentially an orientation with which we approach spiritual life, and therefore it is not always so easy to trace out.

Economic development and sense gratification are concepts that are not difficult to grasp. *Dharma,* however is a complex subject. As *dharma* is a difficult concept to grasp, so mokṣa is an elusive concept. If we go to the root of the meaning of *dharma,* it is apparent that it has little to do with mokṣa. Neither *dharma* as religion for economic development nor *dharma* as religious practice for liberation are pure *dharma.* Therefore, the *Bhāgavata,* while rejecting *kaitava-dharma,* has rejected the pursuit of *mokṣa* in the same verse, *dharmaḥ projjhita kaitavo 'tra.* (SB 1.1.2) *Projjhita* means to reject. While the *Bhāgavata* rejects materialistic religion, it also rejects the idea of rejecting the world, as liberationists advocate. To exploit the world or to reject the world is in the *Bhāgavata's* consideration worldly. The material world runs on two tracks, *bhoga* (enjoyment) and *tyāga* (renunciation). These tendencies correspond with the mentalities of "mine" and "I" respectively. In a crude sense, we try to put ourselves in the center through material acquisition, thinking things are "mine." Persons thus engaged are often so foolish that they may even ask God's help *(kaitava-dharma).* Others, rejecting the personhood of Godhead, think of themselves as the principle of existence, consciousness.

Certainly one can practice religion for economic gain or for salvation, but these are not expressions of pure dharma. Dharma means duty, that which we are bound to do. If we are obliged to do anything, it is to serve. This we cannot avoid. In material life we serve to enjoy the fruits of our labor. In renouncing the world, we try to give up service in order to free ourselves from obligation. Thus both enjoying and renouncing fall short of the true sense of dharma, for both are attempts to move away from that which is our nature. They are artificial, noneternal, and vitiated forms of dharma.

In rejecting the shadow of true eternal *dharma,* the *Bhāgavata* is not criticizing as much as it is advocating something more. The virtues of *dharma* for material gain and *dharma* for liberation are sung throughout the Vedic literature. They are intended to bring one indirectly to essential *dharma.* By first acknowledging God in material pursuit and thereby regulating our material acquisition, we can eventually come to knowledge. Knowledge destroys the impetus for work in a plane where all work is reactionary and binds the soul. Self-knowledge, or self-realization, prepares one for a life of spiritual love, as opposed to a life of material love arising out of ignorance of the spiritual nature of the self. Self-knowledge is our passport to transcendence. Love of God, however, either as a servant of Viṣṇu in Vaikuṇṭha or as a lover of Kṛṣṇa in Vṛndāvana, requires that we get a visa as well. For this an ambassador of grace is our only hope.

If the essential message of the Vedic wisdom is understood by consulting the *Bhāgavata,* we will not get sidetracked by material enjoyment or self-knowledge as we pass through the material plane to the experience of pure self. In this approach, material well-being and liberation are seen as by-products of the culture of *prema-dharma.* Pursued separately, or as ends in themselves, religion for material acquisition and religion for liberation are dead ends for the soul.

Dharma for material gain can lead to knowledge of the futility of material acquisition. This leads to *mokṣa,* which is beyond good and bad material activities *(karma).* But where will we go from there? This is the message of the *Bhāgavata.* The *Bhāgavata* is about the *dharma* of the soul, not about religious duties relative to our material conditioning or mere knowledge of our eternality. It is about *prema-dharma,* our obligation to love the one who has shown so much love for us.

If in postmodern times thoughtful persons are moving away from spirituality that is no more than empty ritual or imitative evangelism, this is progress. In moving away from empty spirituality, many have turned to Eastern traditions. However, many present-day representations of Eastern traditions are also imitative evangelism, although harder to detect as such because they speak to us from within a broader conceptual framework. But whether it be televangelists or mystic magicians or pundits of pedantry, they are all ultimately less than spiritual. They are all *kaitava-dharma.*

Postmodernism's spiritual drift, however, is in the direction of *mokṣa.* It is at best about liberation, and this is not much different than *kaitava-dharma.* It is the other side of the coin of material life, from exploitation and self-inflation to renunciation and self-denial—from narcissism to asceticism. *Prema-dharma* is in the center of these polar opposites. It unites us in a compact of love with the owner of all things and the knower of all there is to be known. Approaching him on friendly terms causes him to share all that he owns and knows. Material well-being *(bhukti)* and knowledge resulting in liberation from karma *(mukti)* are maidservants of devotion *(bhakti).* By devotion Godhead himself is conquered. Any other approach will cause him to hold back, for all other approaches are based on the desire for that which is the property and prerogative of God.

Liberation from the emptiness of material life is a by-product of *prema-dharma,* for knowledge is subordinate to love. *Prema-dharma* turns everything, even so-called material objects and emotions, into an ocean of spiritual experience. We live for love. Learning to love God will enable us to love all things yet be detached from them at the same time, knowing well to whom they belong and thus using them in his service.

Śrī Chaitanya's singing the name of Kṛṣṇa in mass congregations is the most visible expression of *prema-dharma.* This congregational chanting is called *saṅkīrtana. Saṅkīrtana* is derived from two words, *samyak and kīrtana. Samyak* means the most complete, and *kīrtana* is glorification of Godhead. This expression of *prema-dharma* is considered the *yuga-dharma,* or method of approaching transcendence that is most suited for this age (Kali-yuga).

Sound is a powerful medium. According to the Vedas, the world as we know it manifests through sound. From ether (space), to air (movement), to fire (heat), to water (liquidity), to earth (solidity), the physical existence unfolds, all beginning with sound. Because the world is manifested through sound, the *Vedānta-sūtras* tell us *anāvṛittiḥ-śabdaḥ*, that through sound we can disentangle ourselves from the material coverings. Baladeva Vidyābhūṣaṇa's Gauḍīya Vaiṣṇava commentary on the *sūtras* informs us that the sound that disentangles us from material illusion is *kṛṣṇa-saṅkīrtana.* Another great Gauḍīya Vaiṣṇava saint known for his numerable devotional songs, Narottama dāsa, has stated in simple Bengali vernacular, *golokera prema-dhana hari-nāma saṅkīrtana.* "The *saṅkīrtana* of the holy name of Kṛṣṇa has descended from Goloka Vṛndāvana (Kṛṣṇa's transcendental abode)." (Cc. Adi 7.74) Not only can it free us from our material conditioning, it will bring us within a spiritual environment.

Sorting out our material existence is endless. Psychological adjustments can never be a comprehensive approach to properly adjusting our off-center lives. *Kṛṣṇa-saṅkīrtana* is comprehensive because when it is projected into material space, it filters down to all of the other gross elemental constituents of physical existence. It also influences our minds and intelligence, purifying them from distorted sensual input. But more importantly, proper utterance of *kṛṣṇa-saṅkīrtana* is an exercise of the heart. Even its physical *(nāmāparādha)* or mental *(nāmābhāsa)* manifestation can bring about wonderful changes in our lives, from material opulence to liberation respectively. Yet the pure spiritual utterance, sung in a spirit of devotion for its own sake, converts the ego from a spirit of ruling to a spirit of serving. This is a comprehensive solution to our predicament, which arises from misidentification. The holy name of Kṛṣṇa is nondifferent than Kṛṣṇa himself. By purely chanting his name, we properly adjust our position in relation to the actual center.

Śrī Chaitanya taught his followers in his eight stanzas *(Śikśāṣṭakam)* that *kṛṣṇa-saṅkīrtana* is the most generous dispensation of divinity. Chanting the holy name of Kṛṣṇa effectively cleanses the heart of material affinity and eventually grants the devotee entrance into the divine pastimes of Śrī Kṛṣṇa. The name of Kṛṣṇa is beyond rules and regulations. It is Kṛṣṇa himself with all of his potencies *(śaktis).* It can be invoked under any circumstance and benefit will accrue for the chanter. The generosity of Kṛṣṇa's name causes you to feel as though you have no love for the Lord. Devotees should be more humble than a blade of grass, more tolerant than the trees, respectful to others, and not seek honor for themselves. With this attitude, one should chant the name of God incessantly. The opposite sex, wealth, fame, and even liberation from birth and death, are not a concern for the devotee. To be constantly engaged in devotional service should be a devotee's only appeal. To be a particle of dust at the feet of Kṛṣṇa is better than the highest position in the material world. Praying for divine rapture, one will feel separation from Kṛṣṇa and eventually see the world as a void in his absence. Finally the devotee following in the footsteps of Śrī Rādhā should think thus, "Kṛṣṇa may embrace me in love or trample me under his feet. He may break my heart by hiding from me. He may do whatever he likes, but he will always remain the Lord of my life unconditionally."

No one in religious history has better emphasized the essential elements of spiritual life than Śrī Chaitanya. He did so by his personal example. No other *avatāra* has told us more about the nature of the absolute. Christ is said to be the son of God, who died for our sins. His tradition, at best, only hints about God's social life and sexuality. This is certainly a significant contribution. But Śrī Chaitanya's gift is greater. Freedom from sin is a by-product of accepting the divine dispensation of Śrī Chaitanya, who gave us access to the most intimate transcendental pastimes of Godhead, thus enabling us to associate with God beyond awe and reverence. If we are to love God, we must love Śrī Chaitanya, for no one has revealed more about the intimate social life of God. Such revelation provides overwhelming impetus for a life of loving God.

Śrī Chaitanya's book, the *Bhāgavata,* is in one sense a course on comparative religion. All planes of spiritual and material consciousness are objectively discussed therein, such that the reader naturally arrives at the apex of theism in the divine pastimes of Godhead. Śrī Chaitanya did not emphasize a sectarian dogma, but eternal principles of actual spiritual life. The specifics of his divine dispensation therefore must also be taken seriously. After all, there is a definiteness to the absolute that does not compromise its infinity. God has a transcendental name, form, qualities, abode, and pastimes. These aspects of Godhead are most completely expressed in Śrī Chaitanya's Kṛṣṇa conception. Thus to give praise to Kṛṣṇa is complete God worship, because it includes all of these aspects of divinity as no other tradition does.

Support for the scriptural contention that mass prayer is the most effective means for entering into experiential spirituality can be drawn from our experience in the secular world. The *yuga-dharma* expressed in a secular context has been effective in toppling entire political regimes. Most notably, the people of Eastern Europe and the former Soviet Union dethroned communism by taking to the streets in mass congregation, chanting slogans, and waving banners. Similarly, *kṛṣṇa-saṅkīrtana* is most effective for overcoming the oppression of the mind and senses, freeing the soul and issuing in a new world order of love of Godhead.

When Śrī Chaitanya began his *saṅkīrtana* movement in Nadia, West Bengal, he used to chant with his intimate associates three hours nightly. His nocturnal school of kīrtana soon overflowed into the streets, touching thousands of people with the holy name of Kṛṣṇa. Later he stationed himself in the seaside city of Jagannātha Purī. From there he toured throughout India, returning to Purī for his final pastimes. The last twelve years of his life were filled with deep internal spiritual experience. As the name of Kṛṣṇa intoxicated him, he expressed the sentiments of Rādhā's love for Kṛṣṇa in separation with only his most intimate disciples. He set an example for all to follow as to the efficacy of the holy name of Kṛṣṇa properly received from a true saint and chanted sincerely.

The Hare Kṛṣṇa *mahā-mantra* is not a mundane sound. Nor is it a *mantra* intended merely to free the soul from the limits of the mind. It is not to be invoked for material enjoyment, nor is it concerned with world-denying asceticism. For one who approaches the *mahā-mantra* submissively, it will convert the world into an abode of joy, *viśvaṁ pūrnasukāyate.* This was Śrī Chaitanya's vision, *mora man vṛndāvana,* his mind became Vṛndāvana. Thus he dwelled, even while within mortal vision, in the most fundamental causal plane, Vṛndāvana. He saw the sweet will of Kṛṣṇa behind everything. This is what Śrī Chaitanya sought for all—*ānanda moy,* a life of love and joy.

ABOUT THE AUTHOR

Swāmī B. V. Tripurāri was initiated into the Gauḍīya Vaiṣṇava saṁpradāya *(lineage) by A. C. Bhaktivedanta Swami Prabhupāda in 1972. In 1975 in Vṛndāvana, India, he accepted the renounced order of life from Bhaktivedanta Swami and has since become one of his most influential disciples.*

In 1985 Swāmī Tripurāri founded the Gaudiya Vaishnava Society, now an international movement with *āśramas* in the United States, India, and Europe. Since 1988, Swāmī Tripurāri has served as senior editor and publisher of the Clarion Call, an international periodical promoting experiential spirituality. He is the author of numerous articles on the Gauḍīya Vaiṣṇava philosophy and culture. His eagerly-awaited second book, *Ancient Wisdom for Modern Ignorance,* is now in print.

Swāmī Tripurāri travels extensively and can be reached at Śrī Śrī Gaura-Nityananda Audarya Ashrama, 325 River Road, Eugene, OR 97404 USA.

PRONUNCIATION GUIDE

The system of transliteration used in this book conforms to a system that scholars have accepted to indicate the pronunciation of each sound in the Sanskrit language.

The short vowel **a** is pronounced like the **u** in b**u**t, long **ā** like the **a** in f**a**r.

Short **i** is pronounced as in p**i**n, long **ī** as in p**i**que, short **u** as in p**u**ll, and long **ū** as in r**u**le.

The vowel **ṛ** is pronounced like the **ri** in **ri**m, **e** like the **ey** in th**ey**, **o** like the **o** in g**o**, **ai** like the **ai** in **ai**sle, and **au** like the **ow** in h**ow**.

The *anusvāra* (**ṁ**) is pronounced like the **n** in the French word *bo***n**, and *visarga* (**ḥ**) is pronounced as a final **h** sound.

At the end of a couplet, **aḥ** is pronounced **aha**, and **iḥ** is pronounced **ihi**.

The guttural consonants—**k, kh, g, gh,** and **ṅ**—are pronounced from the throat in much the same manner as in English. **K** is pronounced as in **k**ite, **kh** as in Ec**kh**art, **g** as in **g**ive, **gh** as in di**g h**ard, and **ṅ** as in si**ng**.

The palatal consonants—**c, ch, j, jh,** and **ñ**—are pronounced with the tongue touching the firm ridge behind the teeth. **C** is pronounced as in **ch**air, **ch** as in staun**ch-h**eart, **j** as in **j**oy, **jh** as in he**dgeh**og, and **ñ** as in ca**ny**on.

The cerebral consonants—**ṭ, ṭh, ḍ, ḍh,** and **ṇ**—are pronounced with the tip of the tongue turned up and drawn back against the dome of the palate. **Ṭ** is pronounced as in **t**ub, **ṭh** as in ligh**t-h**eart, **ḍ** as in **d**ove, **ḍh** as in re**d-h**ot, and **ṇ** as in **n**ut.

The dental consonants—**t, th, d, dh,** and **n**—are pronounced in the same manner as the cerebrals, but with the forepart of the tongue against the teeth.

The labial consonants—**p, ph, b, bh,** and **m**—are pronounced with the lips. **P** is pronounced as in **p**ine, **ph** as in u**ph**ill, **b** as in **b**ird, **bh** as in ru**b-h**ard, and **m** as in **m**other.

The semivowels—**y, r, l,** and **v**—are pronounced as in **y**es, **r**un, **l**ight, and **v**ine respectively.

The sibilants—**ś, ṣ,** and **s**—are pronounced, respectively, as in the German word **s***prechen* and the English words **sh**ine and **s**un. The letter **h** is pronounced as in **h**ome.

Glossary

ĀCĀRYA—a spiritual master who teaches by example.

ACINTYA-BHEDĀBHEDA—Śrī Chaitanya's doctrine of the "inconceivable oneness and difference" of God and his energies.

ĀDHĀRA-ŚAKTI—God's potency of sustenance.

ADHOKṢAJA—the plane of knowledge that is unapproachable by human effort [God-realization].

ADVAYA-JÑĀNA—nondual knowledge.

ADVAITA—Śaṅkara's philosophy of nondualism.

ADVAITIN—follower of nondualism.

AGAPE—Godly love.

AHIṀSĀ—nonviolence.

ANĀTMAN—"no soul," a tenet of the Buddhist doctrine.

ĀNANDA—spiritual bliss.

ANU—the smallest material particle.

ANUMĀNA—logical conjecture.

APRĀKṚTA—not mundane, although appearing so; applied to the pastimes of Kṛṣṇa.

ĀRĀDHANAM—the highest worship; considered a covert reference to Śrī Rādhā in the *Bhāgavata*.

ARCANĀ—worship of the form of God as manifest in the material elements [deity].

ARTHA—economic development.

ĀSANAS—bodily postures, used in yoga discipline.

ASAT—temporal.

AVATĀRA—"one who descends," a fully or partially empowered incarnation from the spiritual realm for a particular mission.

BHAGAVĀN—possessor of all opulence (God).

BHĀGAVĀTA—the essense of the Vedic literature.

BHOGA—material enjoyment.

BRAHMA-NIRVĀṆA—the goal of the monists (undifferentiated consciousness).

BRĀHMAṆA—a member of the most intelligent class of people, according to the four Vedic occupational divisions of society.

CAKRAS—energy centers of the subtle body.

CIT—cognizance.

DĀSYA-RASA—divine relationship of servitude.

DHARMA—(1) the eternal function of the living entity (to love God). (2) ordinary religion.

DIGVIJAYA—champion scholar.

DVAITA—the philosophy of transcendental duality as espoused by Madhva.

GAUḌĪYA—pertaining to Śrī Chaitanya.

GĀYATRĪ—hymn of the *brāhmaṇas.*

GOLOKA—the supreme planet in the spiritual world.

GOPĪS—the cowherd girlfriends of Śrī Kṛṣṇa in Vṛndāvana, who are his most surrendered and confidential devotees.

GOPĪ-BHĀVA—the transcendental, emotional love exhibited by the *gopīs* for Kṛṣṇa.

GOSWĀMĪ—master of the senses.

HLĀDINĪ-ŚAKTI—the transcendental, internal pleasure potency *(śakti)* of Kṛṣṇa, personified as Śrī Rādhā.

ĪŚVARA—the supreme controller (God).

JAGAT—the material universe.

JAPA—chanting the holy names of God on beads.

JĪVA (JĪVĀTMĀ)—the eternal individual soul.

KAITAVA-DHARMA—cheating materialistic religion.

KALI-YUGA—the current Vedic age characterized by a progressive decline in spiritual knowledge and, consequently, the degeneration of human civilization.

KĀMA—material desire, lust.

KAUSTUBHA—a precious gem that adorns the body of Viṣṇu.

KĪRTANA—singing or speaking in glorification of God.

LĪLĀS—a transcendental "pastime" or activity performed by Godhead.

MĀDHURYA—"sweetness," conjugal love on the spiritual platform.

MAHĀ-MANTRA—the great chant for deliverance.

MAHĀBHĀVA—"great love," the ecstasy of Śrī Chaitanya, shared only by Śrī Rādhā.

MĀYĀ-ŚAKTI—the energy of Godhead that deludes living entities into forgetfulness of their spiritual nature and God.

MOKṢA—liberation from the cycle of birth and death.

MŪRTI—a worshippable form.

NĀMĀBHĀSA—the shadow of the holy name.

NĀMAPARĀDHA—offensive chanting of the holy name.

NARĀYAṆA—Lord of Vaikuṇṭha, known as Viṣṇu.

NASTIKA—an atheist.

NIRĀNANDA—without joy.

NIRGUṆA—without attributes or qualities; in reference to Godhead, the term signifies that he is beyond material qualities.

NYĀYA-ŚĀSTRA—scripture delineating the Vedic school of logic.

PANENTHEISM—the philosophy that all things are within God, but, at the same time, God is not synonymous with all things.

PARAKĪYĀ—"belonging to another," the lawless, transcendental love the *gopīs* exhibit for Kṛṣṇa.

PARAMPARĀ—disciplic succession.

PRAKṚTI—the predominated energies of Godhead of which there are two: the living entities and material nature.

PRĀKṚTA—the mundane world.

PRAMĀṆA—evidence.

PRATYAKṢA—sense perception.

PREMA—pure devotional love for God.

PROJJITAḤ—rejected.

PURĀṆAS—"ancient," 18 supplements to the *Vedas,* which constitute a major portion of the *smṛti.*

PURĀṆIC—from the *Purāṇas.*

PURUṢA—Godhead as the supreme predominator of *prakṛti.*

RĀGĀNUGĀ-BHAKTI—spontaneous devotion, the speciality of the followers of Śrī Chaitanya.

RASA—aesthetic expression of relationship with God in transcendence.

RASARĀJA—king of *rasa,* Kṛṣṇa.

ŚABDA PRAMĀṆA—evidence though divine sound [the *Vedas*].

SĀDHANA—spiritual practice.

SĀDHU—saint.

SAGUṆA—"possessing attributes or qualities," in reference to Godhead, the term signifies that he has spiritual, transcendental qualities.

SĀKHYA—transcendental mood of friendship with Godhead.

SAMPRADĀYA—lineage.

SAṀSĀRA—cycle of birth and death.

SAṄKĪRTANA—congregational glorification of God, especially through the chanting of his holy name.

SANNYĀSA—renounced order of life for spiritual culture.

SANNYĀSĪ—a person in the renounced order.

ŚĀNTA-RASA—divine relationship of equanimity.

SARASWATĪ—the Goddess of learning.

ŚĀSTRA—revealed scripture, Vedic literature.

ŚAKTI—energy.

SIDDHA-DEHA—spiritual body.

SMṚTI—revealed scriptures supplementary to the *Vedas,* such as the *Purāṇas.*

ŚRADDHĀ—faith.

ŚRĪVATSA—imprint.

ŚRUTI—that which is heard [the *Vedas*].

SVAKĪYĀ—"belonging," the transcendental relationship with Kṛṣṇa as a wife.

TAMO-GUṆA—the material mode of ignorance.

TANTRIC—"technique," pertaining to the *tantric* tradition.

ṬĪKĀ—commentary or purport to the scriptures.

TILAKA—clay markings worn on the forehead and other parts of the transcendental body of Viṣṇu, also worn by his devotees.

TĪRTHA—holy place, a place of pilgrimage.

TĀRKĀ—argumentation.

TYĀGA—renunciation.

VAIDHI—regulated devotional practices.

VAIKUṆṬHA—"without anxiety," the eternal planets of the spiritual world.

VAIRĀGYA—detachment.

VAIṢṆAVA—a devotee of Viṣṇu.

VĀTSALYA—the parental mood of affection for Kṛṣṇa.

VEDĀṄGAS—the limbs of the *Vedas.*

VEDĀNTA—"the culmination of knowledge," the philosophical system based on the *Upaniṣads, vedānta-sūtras,* and *Bhagavad-gītā.*

VIŚVAMBHARA—Viṣṇu, the maintainer of the universe, also the childhood name of Śrī Chaitanya.

VIGRAHA—usually the divine image of Godhead, also God's personal form.

VIŚIṢṬĀDVAITA—qualified nondualism, the philosohy of Rāmānuja.

VIṢṆU-MĀYĀ—deluding potency of Viṣṇu.

VRAJA—the transcendental abode of Śrī Kṛṣṇa.

VṚNDĀVANA—Kṛṣṇa's abode.

YAMA-NIYAMA—the ethical basis of yoga, the rules and regulative principles.

BIBLIOGRAPHY

A. C. Bhaktivedanta Swami Prabhupāda. *Bhagavad-gītā As It Is.* Los Angeles: Bhaktivedanta Book Trust, 1985.

——. *The Nectar of Devotion.* London: Bhaktivedanta Book Trust, 1972.

——. *Śrīmad Bhāgavatam.* 30 vols. New York: Bhaktivedanta Book Trust, 1972.

——. *Śrī Caitanya-caritāmṛta.* 17 vols. New York: Bhaktivedanta Book Trust, 1975.

Bainum, David. "Ayurveda and Allopathy: Descending and Ascending Knowledge, A Philosophical Comparison." *Clarion Call,* Vol. 3 No. 1 (1990), p. 37–39.

Bhaktisiddhānta Sarasvatī. *Śrī Brahma-Saṁhitā.* Los Angeles: Bhaktivedanta Book Trust, 1985.

Bhaktivinoda Ṭhākura. *Shri Chaitanya Shikshāmritam.* Madras, India: Sree Gaudiya Math, 1983.

——. *Śrī Chaitanya Mahaprabhu: His Life and Precepts.* Brooklyn, NY: Gaudiya Press, 1987.

Bohm, David. *Wholeness and the Implicate Order.* London: Arc Paperbacks, 1983.

Capra, Fritjof. *The Tao of Physics.* Chicago: Shambala, 1975.

Deadwyler, William. "The Devotee and the Deity: Living a Personalistic Theology," *Gods of Flesh, Gods of Stone: The Embodiment of Divinity in India.* Chambersburg, PA: Anima Books, 1985.

Eck, Diana L. *Darsan: Seeing the Divine Image in India.* Chambersburg, PA: Anima Books, 1981.

Feuerstein, Georg. *Enlightened Sexuality.* Freedom, CA: The Crossing Press, 1989.

Fox, Matthew. *The Coming of the Cosmic Christ.* San Francisco: Harper & Row, 1988.

Śrīla Jīva Gosvāmī. *Śrī Tattva-sandarbha.* Los Angeles: The Kṛṣṇa Institute, 1987.

Sri Rupa Gosvami. *Bhakti-Rasāmṛta-Sindhuh,* Vol. I, trans. Swami B. H. Bon Maharaj. Vrindaban, India: Institute of Oriental Studies, 1965.

Josephson, Brian. " Science and Religion: Can the Two be Synthesized?" *1982–83 Isthamus Foundation Lectures on Science and Religion.* Isthamus Institute, 1982.

Kapoor, O. B. L. *Philosophy and Religion of Śrī Caitanya.* New Delhi, India: Munshiram Manoharlal, 1977.

Narasingha Mahārāja. *Evolution of Theism.* Vṛndāvana, India: GVS, 1989.

Osborn, David, and Thomas Beaudry, "Physics to Metaphysics: A Vedic Paradigm." *Clarion Call,* Vol. 1 No. 3 (1988), pp. 33–37.

Singh, T. D. and Ravi Gomatam, eds. *Synthesis of Science and Religion.* San Francisco: Bhaktivedanta Institute, 1988.

Swami B. H. Bon Maharaj. *My Lectures in England and Germany.* Calcutta, India: Swami B. H. Bon Maharaj, 1984.

Swami B. R. Sridhara. *Golden Volcano of Divine Love.* San Jose, CA: Guardian of Devotion Press, 1984.

——. *The Hidden Treasure of the Sweet Absolute.* Nabadwip, India: Sri Caitanya Saraswat Math, 1985.

——. *Loving Search for the Lost Servant.* San Jose, CA: Guardian of Devotion Press, 1987.

——. *Sermons of the Guardian of Devotion,* Vols. I & II. North Yorkshire, UK: The August Assembly, 1988.

Rupavilasa Dasa. *The Seventh Goswami.* Washington, MS: New Jaipur Press, 1989.

Wilber, Ken. *Holographic Paradigm.* New York: Random Press, 1982.

INDEX